Authority of the Believer

by

A.L. Gill

ISBN 0-941975-31-2

© Copyright 1988, Revised 1995

*Powerhouse Publishing
P.O. Box 99
Fawnskin, CA 92333
(909) 866-3119*

Books by A.L. and Joyce Gill

God's Promises for Your Every Need

Destined for Dominion

Out! In the Name of Jesus

Victory over Deception

Manuals In This Series

The Church Triumphant
Through the Book of Acts

God's Provision for Healing
Receiving and Ministering
God's Healing Power

The Ministry Gifts
Apostle, Prophet, Evangelist,
Pastor, Teacher

Miracle Evangelism
God's Plan to Reach the World

New Creation Image
Knowing Who You Are in Christ

Patterns for Living
From the Old Testament

Praise and Worship
Becoming Worshipers of God

Supernatural Living
Through the Gifts of the Holy Spirit

About the Authors

A.L. and Joyce Gill are internationally known speakers, authors and Bible teachers. A.L.'s apostolic ministry travels have taken him to over fifty nations of the world, preaching to crowds exceeding one hundred thousand in person and to many millions by radio and television.

Their top-selling books and manuals have sold over two million copies in the United States. Their writings, which have been translated into many languages, are being used in Bible schools and seminars around the world.

The powerful life-changing truths of God's Word explode in the lives of others through their dynamic preaching, teaching, writing and video and audio tape ministry.

The awesome glory of the presence of God is experienced in their praise and worship seminars as believers discover how to become true and intimate worshipers of God. Many have discovered a new and exciting dimension of victory and boldness through their teachings on the authority of the believer.

The Gills have trained many believers to step into their own God-given supernatural ministries with the healing power of God flowing through their hands. Many have learned to be supernaturally natural as they are released to operate in all nine gifts of the Holy Spirit in their daily lives and ministries.

Both A.L. and Joyce have Master of Theological Studies degrees. A.L. has also earned a Doctor of Philosophy in Theology degree from Vision Christian University. Their ministry in solidly based on the Word of God, is centered on Jesus, strong in faith and taught in the power of the Holy Spirit.

Their ministry is a demonstration of the Father's heart of love. Their preaching and teaching are accompanied by powerful anointing, signs, wonders, and healing miracles with many being slain in waves under the power of God.

Signs of revival including waves of holy laughter, weeping before the Lord and awesome manifestations of God's glory and power are being experienced by many who attend their meetings.

A Word to Teachers and Students

This powerful study on the **Authority of the Believer** will bring a revelation of restored dominion into the lives of each student. They will learn how to quit losing and start winning in every struggle of life. Believers will be motivated by a fresh revelation of who they are in Jesus Christ. This study will release a boldness and confidence of victory into the lives of the students.

We suggest that before teaching this course you watch or listen to the audio or video tapes on this series and also read the books that are listed as **Suggested Reading.** The more you saturate yourself with the truths of God's Word concerning the authority of the believer and spiritual warfare, the more these truths will move from your mind into your spirit. This manual will then provide the outline for you to use as you impart these truths to others.

Personal life illustrations are a must for effective teaching. The author has omitted these from this work so that the teacher will provide illustrations from his or her own rich experiences, or those of others to which the students will be able to relate.

It should always be remembered that it is the Holy Spirit who has come to teach us all things, and that when we are studying or when we are teaching, we should always be empowered and led by the Holy Spirit.

This study is excellent for personal or group studies, Bible schools, Sunday schools and home groups. It is important that both the teacher and the student have copies of this manual during the course of the study.

The best books are written in, underlined, meditated upon and digested. We have left space for your notes and comments. The format has been designed with a fast reference system for review and to assist you in finding areas again. The special format makes it possible for each person, once they have studied through this material, to teach the contents to others.

Paul wrote to Timothy:

And the things you have heard me say in the presence of many witnesses entrust to reliable men who will also be qualified to teach others. 2 Timothy 2:2b

This course is designed as a practical participation Bible course in the MINDS (Ministry Development System) format which is a specially developed approach to programmed learning. This concept is designed for multiplication in the lives, the ministry and the future teaching of the students. Former students, by using this manual, can teach this course easily to others.

Table of Contents

Suggested Reading for This Course

Destined for Dominion, and
Out! In the Name of Jesus
By A.L. Gill, Powerhouse Publishing

Lesson One

Know Your Enemy

WE ARE AT WAR!

Warfare

As Christians, we must be aware of the fact that we are involved in warfare. One of Satan's main strategies has been to blind our eyes to the conflict we are in, and thus make us defenseless against his attacks. But God has given us every weapon we need to be victorious over our enemy!

2 Corinthians 10:3,4 For though we walk in the flesh, we do not war according to the flesh. For the weapons of our warfare are not carnal but mighty in God for pulling down strongholds.

1 Timothy 6:12 Fight the good fight of faith, lay hold on eternal life, to which you were also called and have confessed the good confession in the presence of many witnesses.

It is important to remember that these weapons are not of the natural world. They are of the spirit.

Many of the writers of the New Testament used terms of warfare. These are not symbolic terms, but rather actual descriptions of the battle in which we are engaged. These battles are to be conducted in the spirit arena.

Our Enemy

We are under attack from the enemy in all areas of our daily lives and relationships – in our:

➤ Families
➤ Finances
➤ Jobs
➤ Minds (mental)
➤ Bodies (health)
➤ Homes
➤ Neighbors
➤ Cities
➤ Nations
➤ World

One of the most important things to learn is that our warfare is not with people. It is against Satan and his evil spirits. It is in the spirit realm. Getting into conflict with people only leads to frustration and defeat.

WHO IS OUR ENEMY?

If we know that we are at war, it is important to establish who our enemy is.

Is our enemy –
➤ Our family?
➤ The people we work with?
➤ Our government?
➤ Our finances?

No!

Rulers – Authorities
Powers – Spiritual Forces

The least in the KOG is equipped to overpower any devil,

The apostle Paul describes our enemy quite graphically. He told us our struggle was not with the people around us. He said we wrestle not against flesh and blood.

Ephesians 6:12 For we do not wrestle against flesh and blood, but against principalities, against powers, against the rulers of the darkness of this age, against spiritual hosts of wickedness in the heavenly places.

The Devil

Peter made it clear that our adversary is the devil.

1 Peter 5:8 Be sober, be vigilant; because your adversary the devil walks about like a roaring lion, seeking whom he may devour.

Schemes

The devil's schemes are his strategies and plans of deception which he uses against us. He has a military-type battle plan to use in his attempt to defeat us. However, as we become aware of his plans, we must become more aware of the armor and weapons that God has provided for our battle. The armor is for our defense. The weapons are for our victorious offense against our enemies.

Ephesians 6:11 Put on the whole armor of God, that you may be able to stand against the wiles of the devil.

A Warning

➤ *Be Occupied with Jesus*
➤ *Know Authority*
➤ *Never be Intimidated by Devil*

We are not to become preoccupied or overly impressed with the devil, his demons, or his schemes. Instead, we are to be occupied with Jesus. As we keep our eyes on Him, we will become aware of who we are in Him. As we become aware of our restored authority through Jesus, a boldness will arise within our spirits. We will not be intimidated by the devil or his schemes.

GOD CREATED ANGELIC BEINGS

God Is Eternal

God is eternal. He has always existed and He is the Creator of all things.

John 1:1-3 In the beginning was the Word, and the Word was with God, and the Word was God. He was in the beginning with God. All things were made through Him, and without Him nothing was made that was made.

John 1:14 And the Word became flesh and dwelt among us, and we beheld His glory, the glory as of the only begotten of the Father, full of grace and truth.

The "Word" is Jesus.

God Created Angels

As the Son of God, Jesus created all things including the angels. They were not only created by Him, but they were created for His divine purpose.

Colossians 1:16,17 For by Him all things were created that are in heaven and that are on earth, visible and invisible, whether thrones or dominions or principalities or powers. All things were created through Him and for Him. And He is before all things, and in Him all things consist.

Angels Are Organized

When Paul listed thrones, dominions, principalities and powers, it was a reference to angels. He used terms that referred to their functions.

They have different titles:
➤ Archangel
➤ Cherubims
➤ Seraphims

> ➤ Living Creatures

They have different functions:
> ➤ Thrones
> ➤ Dominions
> ➤ Principalities
> ➤ Powers

GOD CREATED LUCIFER

Since we know that Jesus created all things, we know that He created Lucifer.

Lucifer's Former Position

Lucifer's original position was one of highest honor. One of his titles was Morning Star.

Isaiah 14:12 How you are fallen from heaven, O Lucifer, son of the morning! How you are cut down to the ground, you who weakened the nations!

Job 38:7 ... when the morning stars sang together, and all the sons of God shouted for joy?

Lucifer's Description

Both the prophet Ezekiel and the prophet Isaiah give us an insight into Lucifer's description.

> ➤ *Model of Perfection*
> ➤ *Full of Wisdom*
> ➤ *Perfect in Beauty*

Ezekiel 28:12b ...Thus says the Lord God: "You were the seal of perfection, full of wisdom and perfect in beauty."

> ➤ *Covered with Jewels*

Ezekiel 28:13a ... every precious stone was your covering: the sardius, topaz, and diamond, beryl, onyx, and jasper, sapphire, turquoise, and emerald with gold.

> ➤ *Beautiful Voice*

Ezekiel 28:13b ...The workmanship of your timbrels and pipes was prepared for you on the day you were created.

Timbrels are the percussion musical instruments. Pipes are the wind instruments such as a flute.

Isaiah 14:11a Your pomp is brought down to Sheol, and the sound of your stringed instruments.

His voice sounded like a great orchestra.

➤ *Blameless*

Ezekiel 28:15 You were perfect in your ways from the day you were created, till iniquity was found in you.

Lucifer's Function

The prophet Ezekiel wrote what Lucifer's original function was.

➤ *Guardian of Throne*

Ezekiel 28:14 You were the anointed cherub who covers; I established you; you were on the holy mountain of God; you walked back and forth in the midst of fiery stones.

Even as the cherubs were on both sides of the mercy seat covering the Ark of the Covenant (Exodus 25:18-22), Lucifer was next to God in the place of greatest honor. As the Morning Star or Son of the Dawn, he covered and protected God's throne and reflected God's radiance and glory. He was anointed as a guardian cherub. He was entrusted by God to the place of greatest responsibility.

➤ *Praise Leader*

From the description of his musical voice, it appears that he led all the angels in their praise and worship of God and that he guarded God's throne with a covering of praise and worship.

WAR IN HEAVEN – LUCIFER'S FALL

Caused by Pride / Rebellion

Understanding Lucifer's rebellion, fall and the resulting warfare in heaven, gives us an understanding of the significance of the warfare that we are now engaged in on earth.

Ezekiel 28:15,17 You were perfect in your ways from the day you were created, till iniquity was found in you.

Your heart was lifted up because of your beauty; you corrupted your wisdom for the sake of your splendor; I cast you to the ground, I laid you before kings, that they might gaze at you.

Lucifer was perfect until he centered his attention on his own beauty instead of on the beauty of the One who had created him. Pride entered. He thought about his own brightness instead of keeping his attention on the radiant brightness of God Himself.

"I Wills"

There was one will, the will of God, that ruled the universe until pride entered into Lucifer.

Isaiah 14:12-17 How you are fallen from heaven, O Lucifer, son of the morning! How you are cut down to the ground, you who weakened the nations! For you have said in your heart:

> **I will ascend into heaven,**
> **I will exalt my throne above the stars of God;**
> **I will also sit on the mount of the congregation on the farthest sides of the north;**
> **I will ascend above the heights of the clouds,**
> **I will be like the Most High.**

Yet you shall be brought down to Sheol, to the lowest depths of the Pit.

Those who see you will gaze at you, and consider you, saying: 'Is this the man who made the earth tremble, who shook kingdoms, who made the world as a wilderness and destroyed its cities, who did not open the house of his prisoners?'

Until this moment there had been only one will in the universe – the will of God. In rebellion, Lucifer exercised his will in opposition to the will of God. As expressed in the five "I wills" of Lucifer, the deception and expression of his rebellion was progressive to the point of attempting to replace God upon the throne in heaven.

The Battle

Revelation 12:7-10 And war broke out in heaven: Michael and his angels fought against the dragon; and the dragon and his angels fought, but they did not prevail, nor was a place found for them in heaven any longer.

➤ *Satan and Angels Cast Out*

So the great dragon was cast out, that serpent of old, called the Devil and Satan, who deceives the whole world; he was cast to the earth, and his angels were cast out with him.

Then I heard a loud voice saying in heaven, "Now salvation, and strength, and the kingdom of our God, and the power of His Christ have come, for the accuser of our brethren, who accused them before our God day and night, has been cast down."

Ezekiel 28:16 By the abundance of your trading you became filled with violence within, and you sinned; therefore I cast you as a profane thing out of the mountain of God; and I destroyed you, O covering cherub, from the midst of the fiery stones.

Lucifer and his angels were cast out of heaven.

Result Of War

One-third of the angels were under Lucifer's command and they fell with him. Other angels, under the command of Michael and Gabriel, remained faithful to God.

➤ *One-Third of Angels Fell*

Revelation 12:4a His tail drew a third of the stars of heaven and threw them to the earth.

Lucifer and "his angels" were flung down to the planet earth.

Revelation 12:9 So the great dragon was cast out, that serpent of old, called the Devil and Satan, who deceives the whole world; he was cast to the earth, and his angels were cast out with him.

➤ *Change of Names*

The names of Lucifer were changed. Where he had been given such lofty titles as Son of the Morning and the Anointed Cherub, his names became:

➤ dragon
➤ serpent
➤ devil
➤ Satan

The angels under Lucifer's authority, those who followed him in rebellion, kept their organizational structure of thrones, powers, rulers, and authorities, but their names were changed to reflect their fallen nature. They were now called demons, devils, evil spirits.

➤ *Change of Nature*

Satan's total nature changed. He was:

➤ the Morning star
➤ the Son of the Dawn
➤ the one who had led praise and worship
➤ the one who guarded and protected the throne of God.

He became:

➤ corrupt
➤ humiliated
➤ outcast from Heaven

He lost:

➤ his great beauty
➤ his high position in the kingdom of God

His nature became:
- dark
- ugly
- evil
- full of hatred

This was all the result of his sins of pride and rebellion.

QUESTIONS FOR REVIEW

1. Describe the original function and position of Lucifer.

2. Describe his rebellion, fall and the warfare that resulted.

3. Who is the real enemy of believers today?

Authority on Earth

EARTH CREATED

By God

In Genesis we are told that God created the earth.

Genesis 1:1 In the beginning God created the heavens and the earth.

➤ *To be Inhabited*

According to Isaiah, the earth was not created to be empty. It was formed to be inhabited.

Isaiah 45:18 For thus says the Lord, Who created the heavens, Who is God, Who formed the earth and made it, Who has established it, Who did not create it in vain, Who formed it to be inhabited: "I am the Lord, and there is no other."

➤ *Became Without Form*

However, Genesis 1:2 describes the earth as without form, void and dark. This description is not of a place ready for habitation. In Hebrew, the word translated into English as "was" could just as accurately be translated as "became."

Genesis 1:2 The earth was (became) without form, and void; and darkness was on the face of the deep. And the Spirit of God was hovering over the face of the waters.

In Jeremiah we find the same Hebrew word used and translated.

Jeremiah 4:23-25 I beheld the earth, and indeed it was (became) without form, and void; and the heavens, they had no light. I beheld the mountains, and indeed they trembled, and all the hills moved back and forth. I beheld, and indeed there was no man, and all the birds of the heavens had fled.

➤ *Became Dark and Empty*

Jeremiah explains that God's judgment turned the perfect earth to a place of destruction (darkness).

Jeremiah 4:23 The earth was without form, and void; and the heavens, they had no light.

Jeremiah went on to describe the judgment of God that was upon the earth.

Jeremiah 4:26,27 I beheld, and indeed the fruitful land was a wilderness, and all its cities were broken down at the presence of the Lord, by His fierce anger.

For thus says the Lord: "The whole land shall be desolate; yet I will not make a full end."

➢ *Satan Came to Earth*

It is possible that Satan was cast down to earth between Genesis 1:1 and Genesis 1:2. (See Note: page 17)

Try to imagine Satan as he was cast to this earth. He had held one of the highest positions in heaven. He had beauty beyond description. He was a reflector of the glory of God. However in his rebellion, he desired even more. He desired to rule in heaven.

There was a battle. He and the angels following him were cast to earth. Everywhere Satan looked he was reminded of the Creator God whom he now hated so much. He was reminded of all that he had lost by his rebellion.

Perhaps Satan, as the one who came to steal, kill, and destroy, in his blind hatred and anger had actually destroyed this earth. The only thing that Satan had left to rule over had become empty, void, and existed in total darkness.

Lucifer had desired to rule over the entire universe. Now, all he had left was one small, dark, empty planet.

Earth Restored by God

In Genesis 1:2, we read that the Spirit of God was hovering over the waters. Genesis 1:3 states that God said "Let there be light." Satan knew that voice!

He had heard it in eternity past. Imagine how he must have panicked when he heard the voice of God. Even here on earth he could not hide from God. Even here, God was not going to leave him alone.

How horrified Satan must have been as he watched God restore the earth to its original beauty in the next five days.

"Then God Said"

The earth was recreated through spoken words. It is important to understand that God spoke back into existence all that had been destroyed.

Genesis 1:3 Then God said, "Let there be light"; and there was light.

v.6 Then God said, "Let there be a firmament in the midst of the waters, and let it divide the waters from the waters."

v.9 Then God said, "Let the waters under the heavens be gathered together into one place, and let the dry land appear"; and it was so.

v.11 Then God said, "Let the earth bring forth grass, the herb that yields seed, and the fruit tree that yields fruit according to its kind, whose seed is in itself, on the earth"; and it was so.

v.14 Then God said, "Let there be lights in the firmament of the heavens to divide the day from the night; and let them be for signs and seasons, and for days and years."

v.20 Then God said, "Let the waters abound with an abundance of living creatures, and let birds fly above the earth across the face of the firmament of the heavens."

v.24 Then God said, "Let the earth bring forth the living creature according to its kind: cattle and creeping thing and beast of the earth, each according to its kind"; and it was so.

v.26 Then God said, "Let Us make man in Our image, according to Our likeness; let them have dominion over the fish of the sea, over the birds of the air, and over the cattle, over all the earth and over every creeping thing that creeps on the earth."

v.29 And God said, "See, I have given you every herb that yields seed which is on the face of all the earth, and every tree whose fruit yields seed; to you it shall be for food."

Satan's Reaction

All that had been perfect, which had been destroyed here on earth, God again made perfect. What was God's plan? Why was God interested in this planet?

Imagine Satan exclaiming to his demons, "Why can't God leave us alone? He has His whole universe to run and all that we have is this one little planet!"

Panic and hatred must have gripped Satan as each day for five days, the voice of God was heard. As God spoke, the earth was restored to its original beauty. The intensity of Satan's hatred toward God must have grown each day.

Note: Bible scholars are not agreed on the sequence of events that relate to Satan's fall and the creation of man. The material in this lesson is based on the "gap theory" which teaches that there is a "gap" in time between verse one and verse two in the first chapter of Genesis. This theory teaches that Satan was cast down to earth after his rebellion and as a result, the earth became formless, empty and dark as described in verse two.

Others teach that Satan's rebellion and fall occurred after man was created. Also, all scholars are not agreed as to the timing of Satan's banishment from heaven to earth.

It is not as important to agree with the sequence of events as described in this lesson, as it is to understand that man, created in God's image, was given absolute authority and dominion on this earth. It is also important to understand that this is the reason why Satan hates mankind so much.

AUTHORITY GIVEN TO MANKIND

Created in God's Image

After God had recreated the earth, He created man and woman in His image. Then He gave them authority over all that was living on the face of the earth.

➤ *Let Them Have Dominion*

In Genesis one, we are told that mankind was created in the image of God. In Genesis nine, we are told the same thing again.

Genesis 1:26 Then God said, "Let Us make man in Our image, according to Our likeness; let them have dominion over the fish of the sea, over the birds of the air, and over the cattle, over all the earth and over every creeping thing that creeps on the earth."

Genesis 9:6 Whoever sheds man's blood, by man his blood shall be shed; for in the image of God He made man.

Knowing that men and women were created in the image of God is important to the understanding of this subject because God's image is one of authority.

Genesis 1:27 So God created man in His own image; in the image of God He created him; male and female He created them.

Given God's Life

God formed the body of man from the dust of the ground with His hands, and then He breathed into him the very breath of God. God breathed into mankind His very nature.

He gave us His life. The life of God is in us!

Genesis 2:7 And the Lord God formed man of the dust of the ground, and breathed into his nostrils the breath of life; and man became a living being.

Authority over Satan

After the war in heaven, Satan had been cast to earth. Can you imagine his horror as he watched God create mankind, breathe into him the very life of God, and then give to this new creation rule and dominion over every living thing on the face of the earth?

Satan was living on the earth! The dominion given to man included authority over Satan and his followers.

Authority Given to Both

God formed Eve and together with Adam, they had authority and dominion over all the things of the earth.

In Genesis 2 we have the story of Eve's creation.

Genesis 2:21-24 And the Lord God caused a deep sleep to fall on Adam, and he slept; and He took one of his ribs, and closed up the flesh in its place.

Then the rib which the Lord God had taken from man He made into a woman, and He brought her to the man.

And Adam said: "This is now bone of my bones and flesh of my flesh; she shall be called Woman, because she was taken out of Man."

Therefore a man shall leave his father and mother and be joined to his wife, and they shall become one flesh.

➤ *Not Just to Adam*

From the first mention of mankind, God said, "Let them have dominion." He did not say "Let him have dominion."

Genesis 1:26-28a Then God said, "Let Us make man in Our image, according to Our likeness; let them have dominion over the fish of the sea, over the birds of the air, and over the cattle, over all the earth and over every creeping thing that creeps on the earth."

So God created man in His own image; in the image of God He created him; male and female He created them.

Then God blessed them, and God said to them, "Be fruitful and multiply; fill the earth and subdue it; have dominion over the fish of the sea, over the birds of the air, and over every living thing that moves on the earth."

Man is not to exercise dominion over woman, nor woman over man, but as one-flesh, they are to walk together in dominion and authority on this earth.

Together, they were given authority over:
➤ The fish of the sea
➤ The birds of the air
➤ The livestock
➤ All the earth
➤ Every living thing

➤ *Not over Other Men*

Man was not to have authority over his fellow man. He was given authority over all of God's creation on this earth and over Satan and his demons. *God Created Satan & Demons*

God now had absolute authority and dominion in all the universe except on planet Earth. Here He had given His authority to these new God-like creatures called man and woman.

Man Given Free Will

➤ *Volition*

God gave Adam a free will. He had the power to choose between obeying and disobeying God. Mankind was given volition, a choice, a free will.

Man's volition was to be tested in the Garden between obedience and disobedience, between eating of the tree of knowledge of good and evil, or not eating of it.

Mankind still has a free will.

Genesis 2:16,17 And the Lord God commanded the man, saying, "Of every tree of the garden you may freely eat; but of the tree of the knowledge of good and evil you shall not eat, for in the day that you eat of it you shall surely die."

SATAN HATES MANKIND

Satan hated Adam and Eve because they were created in God's image. At the moment of their creation, they were given everything he had tried to take by force.

➤ They looked like God.

➤ They talked like God.

➤ They walked like God.

They had been given dominion over all the things on the earth and that included Satan. That included everything he had dominion over. That included all of "his" kingdom.

Satan's Great Fear

Satan knows our authority. He knows what God has said and done.

It is extremely important to him that we do not know our authority – that we do not discover and begin to walk in our God-given authority and dominion. Satan has reason to fear men and women who walk in their God-given authority.

"I Wills" of Satan

Remember the "I wills" of Satan given in Isaiah.

Isaiah 14:13-15 For you have said in your heart:

> **I will ascend into heaven,**
> **I will exalt my throne above the stars of God;**
> **I will also sit on the mount of the congregation on the farthest sides of the north;**
> **I will ascend above the heights of the clouds,**
> **I will be like the Most High.**

Yet you shall be brought down to Sheol, to the lowest depths of the Pit.

Everything Given to Man

Everything Satan willed to be in his rebellion, God created man to be!

➤ Satan said, "I will ascend into heaven."

Mankind was created to have fellowship with God. We were created to walk and talk with the God of this universe! We were created to reign with him."

Revelation 20:6 Blessed and holy are those who have part in the first resurrection. The second death has no power over them, but they will be priests of God and of Christ and will reign with him for a thousand years.

➤ Satan said, "I will exalt my throne above the stars of God."

The stars of God refer to angels. Satan desired to be above the angels in importance.

The apostle Paul wrote that one day we would judge the angels.

1 Corinthians 6:2,3 Do you not know that the saints will judge the world? And if the world will be judged by you, are you unworthy to judge the smallest matters?

Do you not know that we shall judge angels? How much more, things that pertain to this life?

➤ Satan said, "I will also sit on the mount of the congregation on the farthest sides of the north."

We are seated in the heavenly realms in Jesus.

Ephesians 2:6 ... and raised us up together, and made us sit together in the heavenly places in Christ Jesus.

> Satan said, "I will ascend above the heights of the clouds"

We will meet Jesus in the air – in the clouds.

1 Thessalonians 4:16,17 For the Lord Himself will descend from heaven with a shout, with the voice of an archangel, and with the trumpet of God. And the dead in Christ will rise first.

Then we who are alive and remain shall be caught up together with them in the clouds to meet the Lord in the air. And thus we shall always be with the Lord.

> Satan said, "I will be like the Most High."

Man was created in the image of God. Do you still wonder why Satan hates mankind?

We have been created to:
> Look like God
> Talk like God
> Walk like God and
> Rule with God!

How humiliating it must be to Satan that we have been given everything he tried to take in his rebellion.

QUESTIONS FOR REVIEW

1. Explain in your own words the origin of earth, Satan's fall and the resulting judgment of the earth.

2. Describe how God functioned in authority and dominion as He recreated the earth.

3. Explain why Satan hates you. What have you done to cause that hatred?

Lesson Three

Satan's Plan of Deception

Satan saw that Adam and Eve, and thus all mankind, had been given the very same life and nature that God possessed. Satan must have been horrified that mankind now had authority over everything on this earth.

Man looked like God. He acted like God. All the hatred Satan had for God, he turned against man. He could not let man succeed. So, Satan devised his own plan!

SATAN'S PLAN

Deception

Satan had deceived the angels in heaven, and one-third had followed him in rebellion. He was experienced in using deception.

God had given mankind a free will – they could choose to obey or to disobey. With that freedom of choice, He had also given a penalty for disobedience.

Genesis 2:17 ... but of the tree of the knowledge of good and evil you shall not eat, for in the day that you eat of it you shall surely die.

➢ *Disguised Himself*
Questioned God

Satan chose to disguise himself as a serpent so that he could come into the garden unnoticed. He had no right to be in the garden and Adam would have cast him out if Satan had boldly walked in without a disguise.

Genesis 3:1a Now the serpent was more cunning than any beast of the field which the Lord God had made.

"Cunning" means to be sly or crafty.

Satan was within the serpent's body when he talked to Eve. Demons still possess bodies today. That is their disguise and covering for the evil they want to accomplish.

Genesis 3:1b And he said to the woman, "Has God indeed said, 'You shall not eat of every tree of the garden'?"

Satan questioned what God had said, and at the same time left out the penalty for sin.

> *Quoted God*

Notice that Satan quotes God's words in order to twist them into his deception.

Genesis 3:2,3 And the woman said to the serpent, "We may eat the fruit of the trees of the garden; but of the fruit of the tree which is in the midst of the garden, God has said, 'You shall not eat it, nor shall you touch it, lest you die.' "

Eve added "touch" to what God had actually said, but she still remembered the penalty.

> *Satan's Lie*

v.4b "You will not surely die."

Satan contradicted what God had said, but Eve still continued to listen. Then Satan promised a reward for sin.

> *You Will be Like God*

v.5 "For God knows that in the day you eat of it your eyes will be opened, and you will be like God, knowing good and evil."

Satan said to Eve and Adam, "Your eyes will be opened and you'll be like God!" They were already like God but Satan tricked them into wanting more.

ADAM AND EVE SINNED

Both Sinned

Many times, we picture Eve alone when Satan, disguised as a serpent, came to her. That is not what the scripture says. In verse six, we read, "She also gave to her husband with her, and he ate."

They both stopped following God's Words, followed their natural senses, listened to Satan, and ate the fruit.

v.6 So when the woman saw that the tree was good for food, that it was pleasant to the eyes, and a tree desirable to make one wise, she took of its fruit and ate. She also gave to her husband with her, and he ate.

When Adam and Eve disobeyed God and ate the fruit, God's nature left them. They had been clothed in glorious light – the nature of God – now they were naked.

Using the tree of the knowledge of good and evil, Satan had deceived Adam and Eve, tricked and defeated them.

Satan has not changed. His tactics are the same today!

They Were Left

➢ *Defeated*
➢ *Naked*

Satan had deceived them, and mankind was stripped of their covering, dominion and authority.
(the glory of God)

Genesis 3:7 Then the eyes of both of them were opened, and they knew that they were naked; and they sewed fig leaves together and made themselves coverings.

➢ *Afraid*
➢ *Hiding*

Satan had defeated Adam and Eve. Now, the former rulers of this earth were cowering and hiding behind a bush!

Genesis 3:10 So he said, "I heard Your voice in the garden, and I was afraid because I was naked; and I hid myself."

➢ *Still in God's Image*

It is important to understand that even after Adam and Eve sinned they were still made in the image of God. However, they no longer had the life of God in them. They were spiritually dead.

Genesis 9:1,2,6 So God blessed Noah and his sons, and said to them: "Be fruitful and multiply, and fill the earth. And the fear of you and the dread of you shall be on every beast of the earth, on every bird of the air, on all that moves on the earth, and on all the fish of the sea. They are given into your hand."

"Whoever sheds man's blood, by man his blood shall be shed; for in the image of God He made man."

Man was still to:
➢ Be Fruitful
➢ Increase
➢ Fill the earth
➢ Subdue
➢ To have dominion and rule

Now, this would be done in pain, by the sweat of the brow, and all living things would live in dread of mankind.

Review

God had created Adam and Eve to rule this earth. However, when man disobeyed God and exercised his will contrary to God's will, he died spiritually. He was robbed of his God-given authority and dominion.

> *God's will was for men and women*
> *to have authority and dominion.*
>
> *Satan's will was for mankind to rebel against God.*
> *Adam and Eve had a choice to make —*
> *they had a will to exercise —*
> *they aligned their wills with Satan.*
>
> *Satan stole from Adam the titles:*
> *ruler of this world,*
> *the prince of this world.*

AFTER MAN SINNED

Curses That Came

> ➤ *On Serpent*

Since a serpent had allowed Satan to use its body, a curse was placed on all serpents.

Genesis 3:14 So the Lord God said to the serpent: "Because you have done this, you are cursed more than all cattle, and more than every beast of the field; on your belly you shall go, and you shall eat dust all the days of your life."

> ➤ *On Woman*

There were two parts to the curse put on women. She would bear children in pain and man would rule over her.

Genesis 3:16 To the woman He said: "I will greatly multiply your sorrow and your conception; in pain you shall bring forth children; Your desire shall be for your husband, and he shall rule over you."

When a woman accepts Jesus as her personal Savior, she regains her created position. Jesus became the curse for her.

Galatians 3:13 Christ has redeemed us from the curse of the law, having become a curse for us (for it is written, "Cursed is everyone who hangs on a tree").

➤ *On Man*

The curse put on man was that he would toil the ground in pain to secure food.

Genesis 3:17 Then to Adam He said, "Because you have heeded the voice of your wife, and have eaten from the tree of which I commanded you, saying, 'You shall not eat of it': cursed is the ground for your sake; in toil you shall eat of it all the days of your life."

➤ *On Earth*

The earth also was cursed.

vs. 18,19 Both thorns and thistles it shall bring forth for you, and you shall eat the herb of the field. In the sweat of your face you shall eat bread till you return to the ground, for out of it you were taken; for dust you are, and to dust you shall return.

➤ *On Satan*

At the very time Satan gained his great victory over mankind, God pronounced a curse on him.

Genesis 3:15 And I will put enmity between you and the woman, and between your seed and her Seed; He shall bruise your head, and you shall bruise His heel.

God spoke to Satan, who was inside the serpent, and told him that the offspring of the woman would crush his head.

Promise of Redemption!

The curse put on Satan was also the first promise of the coming Messiah. The "Seed" was a prophecy of Jesus who was to be born of a woman.

Satan would be under the feet of Jesus. His head would be crushed and bruised.

Symbols of Future

In the story of the fall of man there are several types, or symbols, of the future.

➤ *Fig Leaf*

The fig leaves that Adam and Eve used to cover themselves are symbols of man's attempt to cover his own sins. They symbolize religions designed by man.

> *Animals Slain*

The first shedding of blood was done by God to cover Adam and Eve. This was a sign, or a type, of Jesus who would be slain as an atonement for the sins of the whole world.

God's Plan

Even at the darkest point in the history of the human race, God had a plan of salvation for mankind.

Jesus Christ, God's Son, of His own free will, would give His life for us.

By His death, He would bring Satan's defeat. Satan would strike Jesus' heel, but Jesus would crush Satan's head. Satan's authority would be crushed and that authority would be restored to man according to God's original plan.

SATAN'S PLAN

Satan's Deception

Satan has never stopped hating and fearing men and women who were created to look and act like God. His plan of deception has never stopped. Through deception, spiritual leaders through the ages have been robbed of their power. They have become blind leaders of the blind.

Satan's Assignments

Satan has organized his forces into a full battle plan. Rulers of darkness are assigned to each nation, each man, woman, and child, to put them into bondage. Their instructions are to steal, kill and destroy.

God brought the law to humanity so that they could have forgiveness for sins and walk in communion with Him. But for four-thousand years Satan lived in dominion over the earth because of mankind's disobedience.

*People created to rule
over this planet were:
blind and begging beside the roads,
bound with spirits of infirmity,
possessed with legions of demons.*

*Faces and bodies, created to look like God,
were eaten away with dreaded leprosy.*

*Men and women created to reign and rule
were living in defeat!*

QUESTIONS FOR REVIEW

1. Explain why Satan so violently hated the creatures called man and woman.

2. Describe the results of man's sin and fall.

3. What was God's promise of redemption as revealed in Genesis 3:15?

Lesson Four

Then Came Jesus – God's Plan

FIRST ADAM – LAST ADAM

God Sent His Son

When Adam and Eve first sinned, God promised to send His Son, the seed of the womam, to crush Satan's head. (Genesis 3:15) Paul tells of this event and relates it to the first promise of a Redeemer.

Galatians 4:4,5 But when the fullness of the time had come, God sent forth His Son, born of a woman, born under the law, to redeem those who were under the law, that we might receive the adoption as sons.

Man's relationship to God and his authority was to be restored by the substitutionary sacrifice that Jesus would make as He died on the cross.

Redeemed from sin, its penalty, and the resulting curse from the law, man could be born again into the family of God. He could become a new creation. He could once again, receive God's Spirit within himself.

Adam Brought Sin

Sin came into this world through the disobedience of Adam.

Romans 5:12 Therefore, just as through one man sin entered the world, and death through sin, and thus death spread to all men, because all sinned ...

Jesus Brought

➤ *Righteousness*

Through the total obedience of one man, Jesus, many could become righteous.

v.19 For as by one man's disobedience many were made sinners, so also by one Man's obedience many will be made righteous.

➤ *Good News*

After Adam and Eve sinned, when they knew God was coming, they hid behind the bushes. Now Jesus, the Son of God was coming and the angels said, "Don't be afraid! This is good news for you."

Luke 2:10,11 Then the angel said to them, "Do not be afraid, for behold, I bring you good tidings of great joy which will be to all people. For there is born to you this day in the city of David a Savior, who is Christ the Lord."

➤ *Peace to Men*

One angel began the message to the shepherds on the Bethlehem hillside that night, but the joy in heaven was so great, the spirit realm burst into the natural realm.

vs.13,14 And suddenly there was with the angel a multitude of the heavenly host praising God and saying: "Glory to God in the highest, and on earth peace, good will toward men!"

What a wonderful promise was given, even as Christ was born. "On earth peace, good will toward men"

There are no words to describe the joy
felt throughout the whole universe.
The angels
were so excited
they burst into open view of the shepherds
to sing their praises.
Even the stars proclaimed His birth!

JESUS OPERATED ON THIS EARTH AS A MAN!

Did Jesus operate in authority and power while on this earth as God, or as a man – empowered by the Holy Spirit?

Jesus, the Last Adam

Paul referred to Jesus as the Last Adam.

1 Corinthians 15:45 And so it is written, "The first man Adam became a living being." The last Adam became a life-giving spirit.

Jesus, as the Last Adam, walked and ministered in authority on this earth even as He had created the first Adam to do.

It is very important to understand this because it was only by fulfilling the law as the Last Adam that He could bring us freedom from the law. Only by being human could He become our Savior. It was necessary that He defeat Satan, as a man, to win back the authority that Satan had stolen from the first Adam.

Since Jesus was the first perfect man since Adam, He had the authority given to Adam. When the Holy Spirit came upon Him, He also had the power of God within Him.

Baptism of Jesus

➤ *Spirit Came on Him*

John the Baptist saw the Spirit of God descend on Jesus and this event was so important that it was recorded in all four Gospels (Mark 1:10, Luke 3:22, John 1:32).

Matthew 3:16 Then Jesus, when He had been baptized, came up immediately from the water; and behold, the heavens were opened to Him, and He saw the Spirit of God descending like a dove and alighting upon Him.

➤ *Miracles Performed*

Jesus had performed no miracles through the first thirty years of His life, but when He was to begin His public ministry the Holy Spirit came upon Him. Then, in the power of the Holy Spirit, Jesus' miracle ministry began.

The authority of God operating with the Spirit of God are the power twins of victory!

Jesus Gave up Rights as God

➤ *He Emptied Himself*

The apostle Paul gives us an insight into the mind of Christ as He came to this earth. Paul wrote that Jesus laid aside all His attributes as God.

Philippians 2:5-8 Let this mind be in you which was also in Christ Jesus, who, being in the form of God, did not consider it robbery to be equal with God, but made Himself of no reputation, taking the form of a servant, and coming in the likeness of men. And being found in appearance as a man, He humbled Himself and became obedient to the point of death, even the death of the cross.

Jesus willed to:
➤ Make Himself of no reputation
➤ Take the form of a servant
➤ Come in likeness of man
➤ To humble Himself

> ➤ Become obedient to death

Jesus had the nature of God, and was equal with God and yet, He emptied Himself of all His rights as God, to function on this earth as a man. He took on Himself the form of a servant and the likeness and appearance of a man. He humbled Himself and became obedient to death. He came to this earth as a man and His power on this earth would come through the Holy Spirit.

Why was this important?

Adam, the first man, had disobeyed God and surrendered his authority to Satan. Jesus, as the Last Adam, would do everything on this earth as a man empowered by the Spirit of God. He would be the perfect man operating on this earth as Adam had been created to do.

As Son of Man

While Jesus was on this earth, the authority He operated in was as the Son of Man. In the following passage, John used a very exact choice of words: "Son of God" – "Son of Man."

John 5:25-27 Most assuredly, I say to you, the hour is coming, and now is, when the dead will hear the voice of the Son of God; and those who hear will live. For as the Father has life in Himself, so He has granted the Son to have life in Himself, and has given Him authority to execute judgment also, because He is the Son of Man.

The dead would hear the voice of the Son of God. Outside of this earth, Jesus operated as part of the triune God-Head.

On this earth, Jesus walked in authority because He was the Son of Man. Man was created to walk with authority and dominion. It was the human Jesus who had authority. It was because He was the Son of Man, the Last Adam, not because He was the Son of God.

If Jesus Did It, We Can Do It Too!

Jesus did only what man was created originally to do on earth. He moved in the power of the Holy Spirit, and not in the power of the **Son of God!**

This is very important to us! If Jesus operated as a man on this earth, then we can do the same things He did. We have the same power, authority, and right to do everything that Jesus did when He was here on earth as a **Man**.

FACED TEMPTATION AS A MAN

Tempted as We

God had given Adam and Eve a free will, a choice, a volition. Jesus had this same volition. To be completely the Last Adam, Jesus had to suffer temptation also.

Adam and Eve were tempted in three areas:

➢ **Body** – Eve saw the fruit, that it was good for food.

➢ **Soul** – Satan promised her wisdom, knowing good from evil.

➢ **Spirit** – Finally he promised her she would be like God.

Jesus was tempted in these three areas also.

First Temptation – Body

Jesus had been in the wilderness for forty days. Satan tried, in this time of physical weakness, to tempt Jesus into using His powers as the Son of God to satisfy the needs of his human body. But Jesus had laid aside the attributes of God when He came to this earth to operate as the Son of Man.

➢ *Satisfy Human Needs*

Matthew 4:1-3 Then Jesus was led up by the Spirit into the wilderness to be tempted by the devil. And when He had fasted forty days and forty nights, afterward He was hungry. Now when the tempter came to Him, he said, "If You are the Son of God, command that these stones become bread."

When the tempter came to Him, he said, "If you are the Son of God, prove yourself, take back your rights as God. If You are the Son of God, command that these stones become bread."

If Jesus had turned the stones to bread, He would not have been operating as a man. He would have been using His attributes as God. If He had done that, Satan would have defeated both the first Adam and the Last Adam.

➢ *Jesus Answered*

Jesus answered Satan by quoting the Word of God.

Matthew 4:4 But He answered and said, "It is written, 'Man shall not live by bread alone, but by every word that proceeds from the mouth of God.'"

Notice that Jesus identified Himself as a man.

v.5 Then the devil took Him up into the holy city, set Him on the pinnacle of the temple.

Second Temptation – Soul

The second temptation was in the area of the soul. Satan tempted Jesus to reason contrary to God's will for His life and to act on His emotions.

➤ *Prove Yourself*

v.6 ... and said to Him, "If You are the Son of God, throw Yourself down. For it is written: 'He shall give His angels charge concerning you,' and, 'In their hands they shall bear you up, lest you dash your foot against a stone.' "

This was a continuation of the same basic temptation. "If you are the Son of God ..." Satan knew He was the Son of God. Jesus' life on this earth was to be lived as the Son of Man, the Last Adam.

➤ *Jesus Answered*

Jesus defeated Satan by correctly speaking the Word of God. Jesus knew He was Lord and Satan knew it.

v.7 Jesus said to him, "It is written again, 'You shall not tempt the Lord your God.' "

Third Temptation – Spirit

In the third temptation, Satan offered Jesus all the kingdoms of this world. Wasn't that the reason Jesus had come to this earth? Wasn't He here to win back the earth from Satan?

➤ *Be God of this World*

Matthew 4:8,9 Again, the devil took Him up on an exceedingly high mountain, and showed Him all the kingdoms of the world and their glory. And he said to Him, "All these things I will give You if You will fall down and worship me."

Satan did have the right to offer these kingdoms to Jesus. Satan, having deceived and robbed Adam of his authority, was then the ruler of this earth.

But Jesus was not interested in taking the earth back from Satan in any manner that would be in disobedience to the Father.

➤ *Jesus Answered*

Jesus did not enter into a debate with Satan. He did not argue with him over who ruled this world. Jesus told him to leave. He spoke the Word of God again.

Matthew 4:10 Then Jesus said to him, "Away with you, Satan! For it is written, 'You shall worship the Lord your God, and Him only you shall serve.'"

Review

If Jesus had acted as the Son of God as Satan tempted Him to do, He would have given up His rights as the Son of Man. He would no longer have been qualified to be the perfect Substitute to provide for mankind's redemption.

Satan offered to Jesus the very thing He had come to win back – the right to rule this earth. It would have been so "easy" to do it Satan's way – no death on the cross. Jesus knew that without the shedding of His blood there would be no remission of sin.

Even as Jesus was dying on the cross, Satan, through people, mocked Jesus with the same words.

Matthew 27:40 ...You who destroy the temple and build it in three days, save Yourself! If You are the Son of God, come down from the cross.

Often, Satan will offer us the very things God has promised us. All we must do is compromise in some area. Our method of winning over his strategies is to know and speak the Word of God.

JESUS, OUR EXAMPLE IN RESISTING TEMPTATION

Jesus Understands Temptation

As the story of Jesus' temptation is related in Matthew we are given the opportunity to learn how Satan is to be defeated in this area. We also have free choice. We also will be tempted, but as Jesus walked away in victory – so can we!

Paul states that since Jesus has suffered by being tempted, He is able to help those who are being tempted.

Hebrews 2:18 For in that He Himself has suffered, being tempted, He is able to aid those who are tempted.

Jesus Tempted as We

We can experience a bold confidence by knowing that Jesus was tempted in every area just as we may be. As He did not yield to that temptation, we too can go to God and obtain His supernatural help to withstand the temptation.

Hebrews 4:14-16 Seeing then that we have a great High Priest who has passed through the heavens, Jesus the Son of God, let us hold fast our confession. For we do not have a High Priest who

cannot sympathize with our weaknesses, but was in all points tempted as we are, yet without sin. Let us therefore come boldly to the throne of grace, that we may obtain mercy and find grace to help in time of need.

All Temptations Common

One of Satan's strategies is to make us feel that we are different, that our temptation is unique, or harder than what others suffer. But all temptations are common and God has given us a way of escape so that we can stand up under it.

1 Corinthians 10:13 No temptation has overtaken you except such as is common to man; but God is faithful, who will not allow you to be tempted beyond what you are able, but with the temptation will also make the way of escape, that you may be able to bear it.

Follow Jesus' Example

Jesus is our example. Just as Jesus answered Satan by using the Word of God, we are to do the same.

When Satan came to Jesus, Jesus did not
➢ argue with Satan
➢ reason with Satan
➢ consider doing it Satan's way

Jesus quoted the written Word of God.

Matthew 4:4 But He answered and said, "It is written, 'Man shall not live by bread alone, but by every word that proceeds from the mouth of God.' "

This is how Satan is defeated. The Word of God must flow out of our mouths.

When disease tries to come on our bodies, we can say, "It is written, 'By His stripes I am healed.'"

When poverty tries to come against our finances, we can say, "It is written, 'My God shall supply all my needs ...'"

When Satan tries to lead our children astray, we can say, "It is written, 'All my children shall be taught of the Lord...'"

Speak the solution — not the problem.

Speak the answer — not the need.

Speak and believe the Word of God,

and Satan will be:

totally,

completely,

utterly,

defeated!

And you will be victorious!

QUESTIONS FOR REVIEW

1. Why is it important for you to know that Jesus gave up His rights as God and lived and operated as a man while He was on the earth?

2. What example can you give of Jesus operating in the authority of a man while He was on earth?

3. Following Jesus' example, how can you best defeat Satan or his demons when they try to tempt you to disobey God?

Jesus Ministered with Authority

GOD'S PLAN FOR ALL BELIEVERS

Jesus, as Man

Jesus operated on this earth as a man. He had purposefully emptied Himself of His rights as God. He suffered temptations as a man. He overcame Satan as a man.

It was the human Jesus who had authority on this earth. His authority was because He was the Son of Man, the Last Adam, not because He was the Son of God.

Jesus came as the Last Adam to fulfill all that God had created the first Adam to be. Fulfilling God's plan for the first Adam, Jesus walked in absolute authority and dominion on this earth.

It is important to understand the authority in which Jesus walked. If this authority was the authority that God, at creation, had given to mankind, then we can also walk in the same authority as redeemed men and women today.

Luke 10:19 Behold, I give you the authority to trample on serpents and scorpions, and over all the power of the enemy, and nothing shall by any means hurt you.

Only as new creations in Jesus can we become the men and women that we were created to be in God's plan. Only as we read the Gospels and see Jesus walking as a perfect man can we understand God's pattern for our living and walking in absolute authority and dominion every day of our lives.

LUKE TELLS OF JESUS' AUTHORITY

First Message

➤ *"In Power of Holy Spirit"*

When Jesus was baptized in the Jordan River, the Holy Spirit came upon Him to empower Him for His earthly ministry. Immediately after this, He was led into the wilderness, where He won over Satan and his temptations by speaking the Word of God. Having demonstrated His authority on this earth as a man empowered by the Holy Spirit, He was ready for His earthly ministry to begin.

He began this ministry in Galilee, anointed by the power of the Holy Spirit and speaking with authority.

Luke 4:14,16,18-21 Then Jesus returned in the power of the Spirit to Galilee, and news of Him went out through all the surrounding region.

So He came to Nazareth, where He had been brought up. And as His custom was, He went into the synagogue on the Sabbath day, and stood up to read.

"The Spirit of the Lord is upon Me, because He has anointed Me to preach the gospel to the poor. He has sent Me to heal the brokenhearted, to preach deliverance to the captives and recovery of sight to the blind, to set at liberty those who are oppressed, to preach the acceptable year of the Lord."

Then He closed the book, and gave it back to the attendant and sat down. And the eyes of all who were in the synagogue were fixed on Him. And He began to say to them, "Today this Scripture is fulfilled in your hearing."

(Jesus was reading Isaiah 61:1,2)

Second Message

After Jesus spoke in Nazareth, He spoke in Capernaum. There the people were amazed at His authority.

➤ *Had Authority*

Luke 4:31,32 Then He went down to Capernaum, a city of Galilee, and was teaching them on the Sabbaths. And they were astonished at His teaching, for His word was with authority.

➤ *Demon Cast Out*

vs.33-35 Now in the synagogue there was a man who had a spirit of an unclean demon. And he cried out with a loud voice, saying, "Let us alone! What have we to do with You, Jesus of Nazareth? Did You come to destroy us? I know You, who You are—the Holy One of God!"

But Jesus rebuked him, saying, "Be quiet, and come out of him!" And when the demon had thrown him in their midst, it came out of him and did not hurt him.

Jesus commanded the demon to come out, and because it knew Jesus' authority, it came out.

➤ *"Authority and Power"*

v.36 So they were all amazed and spoke among themselves, saying, "What a word this is! For with authority and power He commands the unclean spirits, and they come out."

JESUS' AUTHORITY OVER DEMONS – SICKNESS – TREES – STORMS

Mark also wrote about the ministry of Jesus in Capernaum and the people's amazement over the authority in which He ministered. Mark went on to tell about other demon possessed and sick people being healed.

Authority over Demons

Jesus had authority over the demons.

vs.40,41 Now when the sun was setting, all those who had anyone sick with various diseases brought them to Him; and He laid His hands on every one of them and healed them. And demons also came out of many, crying out and saying, "You are the Christ, the Son of God!" And He, rebuking them, did not allow them to speak, for they knew that He was the Christ.

Authority over Illness

Jesus had authority over illness.

Mark 1:40,41 Then a leper came to Him, imploring Him, kneeling down to Him and saying to Him, "If You are willing, You can make me clean."

And Jesus, moved with compassion, put out His hand and touched him, and said to him, "I am willing; be cleansed."

Authority over Human Body

Jesus spoke to the man with a shriveled hand. "Stretch out your hand!"

Mark 3:1-3 And He entered the synagogue again, and a man was there who had a withered hand. And they watched Him closely, whether He would heal him on the Sabbath, so that they might accuse Him. Then He said to the man who had the withered hand, "Step forward."

Jesus knew the man was going to be healed. He said, "Step forward."

vs4,5 And He said to them, "Is it lawful on the Sabbath to do good or to do evil, to save life or to kill?" But they kept silent. So when He had looked around at them with anger, being grieved by the hardness of their hearts,

He said to the man, "Stretch out your hand." And he stretched it out, and his hand was restored as whole as the other.

With authority, Jesus spoke a word and the man stretched out his hand and was healed.

Authority over Creation

➤ *Cursed Fig Tree*

Jesus had authority over the fig tree.

Matthew 21:19 And seeing a fig tree by the road, He came to it and found nothing on it but leaves, and said to it, "Let no fruit grow on you ever again." And immediately the fig tree withered away.

Authority over Elements

➤ *Calmed Storm*

Jesus spoke to the wind and sea with authority and they obeyed Him.

Mark 4:35-38 On the same day, when evening had come, He said to them, "Let us cross over to the other side."

Now when they had left the multitude, they took Him along in the boat as He was. And other little boats were also with Him. And a great windstorm arose, and the waves beat into the boat, so that it was already filling. But He was in the stern, asleep on a pillow. And they awoke Him and said to Him, "Teacher, do You not care that we are perishing?"

Jesus rebuked the wind and spoke to the sea.

vs.39,40 Then He arose and rebuked the wind, and said to the sea, "Peace, be still!" And the wind ceased and there was a great calm.

But He said to them, "Why are you so fearful? How is it that you have no faith?"

Jesus' implication was, "Why were you so afraid? You could have calmed the storm. Where is your faith?"

v.41 And they feared exceedingly, and said to one another, "Who can this be, that even the wind and the sea obey Him!"

JESUS, OUR EXAMPLE

Jesus is our example of how we should walk and minister in authority. His works on earth as the Last Adam are an example of how we, as redeemed and restored mankind, are to do the works of Jesus on the earth today. We are to live and minister in the same bold authority that Jesus did as we do His works.

John 14:12 Most assuredly, I say to you, he who believes in Me, the works that I do he will do also; and greater works than these he will do, because I go to My Father.

Jesus Rebuked Fever

Jesus spoke with authority when He rebuked the fever in Peter's mother-in-law.

Luke 4:38,39 Now He arose from the synagogue and entered Simon's house. But Simon's wife's mother was sick with a high fever, and they made request of Him concerning her. So He stood over her and rebuked the fever, and it left her. And immediately she arose and served them.

Raising of Lazarus

Jesus spoke boldly and forcibly in a loud voice at the grave of Lazarus.

John 11:43 Now when He had said these things, He cried with a loud voice, "Lazarus, come forth!"

Doing Works of Jesus

Everywhere Jesus went, He ministered with a boldness that came as a result of knowing His authority as the Son of Man. When He released that authority in the power of the Holy Spirit, He healed the sick, cast out demons and raised the dead. He did it as an example for believers both in that day and in our day.

Jesus told the disciples to minister in that same authority and to do exactly the same works that He had been doing.

Matthew 10:8 Heal the sick, cleanse the lepers, raise the dead, cast out demons. Freely you have received, freely give.

The disciples could do the works of Jesus because He had given them the same authority in which He lived and ministered.

Luke 10:19 Behold, I give you the authority to trample on serpents and scorpions, and over all the power of the enemy, and nothing shall by any means hurt you.

Bold Authority

Jesus' ministry provided an example of boldness and power, instead of fear and timidity.

2 Timothy 1:7 For God has not given us a spirit of fear, but of power and of love and of a sound mind.

Jesus boldly preached the gospel, cast out devils and laid His hands on sick people and saw them recover as He ministered with authority. Jesus, our example, left us with these parting words.

Mark 16:15-18 And He said to them, "Go into all the world and preach the gospel to every creature. He who believes and is baptized will be saved; but he who does not believe will be condemned.

"And these signs will follow those who believe: in My name they will cast out demons; they will speak with new tongues; they will take up serpents; and if they drink anything deadly, it will by no means hurt them; they will lay hands on the sick, and they will recover."

When we follow Jesus' example, as the Last Adam, we will find ourselves obeying the words of Jesus, as the creator, to the first Adam. We will find ourselves ruling and taking dominion over this earth and everything on this earth including sickness, bondage, poverty and death. Once again we will be doing what we were created to do.

Satan's Horror

As Jesus ministered on this earth, Satan must have looked on in horror. Here, Jesus operating as a man, was taking dominion, speaking and ministering in authority and by so doing was destroying the works of Satan.

1 John 3:8b For this purpose the Son of God was manifested, that He might destroy the works of the devil.

As we follow the example of Jesus today, we too will live and minister in our God-given authority. We too will be destroying the devil's work.

QUESTIONS FOR REVIEW

1. According to John 5:25-27, did Jesus operate in authority as the Son of God, or as the Son of Man?

2. Give examples of Jesus walking in authority over the elements, over sickness and disease, and over demon spirits.

3. What was the reaction of people to Jesus acting in authority on this earth?

4. What might be the reaction of people today when you walk in authority on this earth?

Lesson Six

From the Cross to the Throne

DEATH OF JESUS

Satan's kingdom was being destroyed, and Satan knew that Jesus must be killed. Deception had worked with the angels. It had worked against Adam and Eve. But it had not worked against Jesus!

However, once again, Satan used deception. He deceived the religious leaders of that day into demanding Jesus' death. He possessed the body of Judas to accomplish the betrayal even as he had entered the body of the serpent to accomplish the deception of Adam and Eve.

Satan hated Jesus so much that not only did he want Him dead, he wanted Him tormented. All of Satan's principalities, powers, rulers of darkness, and wicked spirits came to gloat. They must have been preparing for their moment of greatest victory and celebration when their own destruction came.

Jesus was betrayed, beaten, crucified.

Great Deceiver, Deceived

Satan, the great deceiver was himself deceived. In his blind hatred, he did not realize that he had just caused the death of the Person who would, by that death and subsequent resurrection, utterly defeat him and redeem mankind from the results of their sin.

Jesus paid the price for our sin by dying on the cross.

He delivered all of our sins, sicknesses, diseases and infirmities to the place of torments. When all the sin of this world was removed from Jesus, the power of God came on Him. The whole world shook during this time of great spiritual warfare. Jesus spoiled Satan and his demons. Satan, since the time of Adam, had been holding men under his authority. Jesus took the keys of authority away from the devil.

WHAT HAPPENED ON EARTH?

There were three days of battle. Jesus had said that as Jonah was three days and three nights in the belly of the whale, He would be three days and three nights in the heart of the earth.

Matthew 12:40 For as Jonah was three days and three nights in the belly of the great fish, so will the Son of Man be three days and three nights in the heart of the earth.

➤ *Veil Torn in Two*
➤ *Earth Shook*
➤ *Rocks Split*
➤ *Tombs Opened*

No longer were men to be separated from God. The veil in the temple, into the Holy of Holies, was torn in two. The earth shook violently as Jesus broke the bands of death in the heart of the earth.

Matthew 27:50-53 Jesus, when He had cried out again with a loud voice, yielded up His spirit. And behold, the veil of the temple was torn in two from top to bottom; and the earth quaked, and the rocks were split, and the graves were opened; and many bodies of the saints who had fallen asleep were raised; and coming out of the graves after His resurrection, they went into the holy city and appeared to many.

WHAT HAPPENED IN SPIRIT WORLD?

The battle was joined between Jesus, our Substitute, and Satan with his demonic hosts.

While Jesus was being nailed to the cross, Satan must have summoned all of his demons to witness this crucial event. This was too important for any of them to miss! As Jesus died on the cross, Satan and his demons must have been preparing in fiendish glee for what they thought would be their greatest moment of triumph.

It was not enough for Satan to see Jesus' lifeless body hanging on the cross. In blind hatred, Satan must have shouted, "He must be cast into the depths of Hades!" Satan and his demons in their ignorant folly must have begun an exhilarated, but short lived celebration as the gates of Hell slammed shut behind Jesus.

Jesus, loaded with the horrible sins of all mankind, suffered all the torments of Hades as He helplessly descended to the depths of the bottomless pit. There, He stooped and delivered every sin that was or ever would be committed. He buried all of our sins to be remembered no more.

Psalms 103:12 As far as the east is from the west, so far has He removed our transgressions from us.

Foretold by David

> ➤ *Bore Penalty of Sin*
> ➤ *Bore Judgment of Sin*

David described what happened to Jesus after His death. Bearing our sins, He seemed helpless as Satan planned His final destruction. He descended to the deepest part of Hades. Here, those who had died in unbelief were held in torment and judgment.

Jesus went to hell, bearing the penalty and judgment of our sins.

Psalms 88:3-7 I am counted with those who go down to the pit; I am like a man who has no strength, adrift among the dead, like the slain who lie in the grave, Whom You remember no more, and who are cut off from Your hand.

You have laid me in the lowest pit, in darkness, in the depths.

David also prophesied about the resurrection of Jesus.

Psalms 16:10 For You will not leave my soul in Sheol, nor will You allow Your Holy One to see corruption.

Foretold by Isaiah

The prophet Isaiah foretold the death and resurrection of Jesus.

Isaiah 53:8-12 He was taken from prison and from judgment, and who will declare His generation? For He was cut off from the land of the living; for the transgressions of My people He was stricken. And they made His grave with the wicked—but with the rich at His death, because He had done no violence, nor was any deceit in His mouth.

Yet it pleased the Lord to bruise Him; He has put Him to grief. When You make His soul an offering for sin, He shall see His seed, He shall prolong His days, and the pleasure of the Lord shall prosper in His hand.

He shall see the travail of His soul, and be satisfied. by His knowledge My righteous Servant shall justify many, for He shall bear their iniquities.

Lamb of God

➤ *Bore Sins of Many*
➤ *Interceded for Transgressors*

Therefore I will divide Him a portion with the great, and He shall divide the spoil with the strong, because He poured out His soul unto death, and He was numbered with the transgressors, and He bore the sin of many, and made intercession for the transgressors.

On the cross, Jesus fulfilled the function of the sacrificial lambs of the Old Testament.

John 1:29 The next day John saw Jesus coming toward him, and said, "Behold! The Lamb of God who takes away the sin of the world!"

Scapegoat

As Jesus bore our sins to the depths of the earth, He fulfilled the function pictured by the scapegoat which bore away the sins of the people.

Leviticus 16:10,21,22 But the goat on which the lot fell to be the scapegoat shall be presented alive before the Lord, to make atonement upon it, and to let it go as the scapegoat into the wilderness.

And Aaron shall lay both his hands on the head of the live goat, confess over it all the iniquities of the children of Israel, and all their transgressions, concerning all their sins, putting them on the head of the goat, and shall send it away into the wilderness by the hand of a suitable man. The goat shall bear on itself all their iniquities to an uninhabited land; and he shall release the goat in the wilderness.

JESUS COULD NOT BE HELD!

When Jesus delivered our sins into the deepest part of the pit, the power of God came upon Him.

Acts 2:27 ... because You will not leave my soul in Hades, nor will You allow Your Holy One to see corruption.

The gates of hell (Hades) could not prevail against Jesus. Breaking through the gates of hell, He snatched the keys of death, hell and the grave away from Satan.

Devil and Demons Defeated

The history of ancient battles and the defeat of the enemies gives special insight into the significance of the following verse.

Colossians 2:15 Having disarmed principalities and powers, He made a public spectacle of them, triumphing over them in it.

Powers and authorities, as we have studied before, are references to Satan's organization of demons.

In ancient times, when an army defeated their enemy, they disarmed them, stripped off their clothes, bound them in chains one to another, and in total dishonor marched them back, as slaves, to the conquering nation.

Jesus personally disarmed Satan and every demon. He took their weapons away from them. He stripped off their clothes. He made a public spectacle of them.

Those who days earlier were celebrating as Jesus hung stripped, naked and humiliated on the cross, were now humiliated in like manner.

Satan defeated Adam and Eve
➢ left them naked,
➢ stripped of their authority.

Satan thought he had defeated Jesus
➢ and left Him stripped, naked
➢ hanging on the cross.

However, Jesus defeated Satan and his demons
➢ left them naked,
➢ stripped of their authority for all eternity!

The Resurrection

Having paid the penalty of sin by His death on the cross and delivering our sins to the depths of the pit, Jesus took the keys of death, hell and the grave away from Satan.

Having defeated Satan and broken his power over death, the tomb could no longer hold Jesus' body. In an explosion of powerful triumph, Jesus arose from the dead. Satan and every demon had been defeated!

Ephesians 1:19-21 ... and what is the exceeding greatness of His power toward us who believe, according to the working of His mighty power which He worked in Christ when He raised Him from the dead and seated Him at His right hand in the heavenly places, far above all principality and power and might and dominion, and every name that is named, not only in this age but also in that which is to come.

JESUS ASCENDED

In Triumph

Jesus triumphantly ascended back to heaven and He led captives in His train.

Ephesians 4:8-10 Therefore He says: "When He ascended on high, He led captivity captive, and gave gifts to men."

(Now this, "He ascended"–what does it mean but that He also first descended into the lower parts of the earth? He who descended is also the One who ascended far above all the heavens, that He might fill all things.)

When Jesus led captivity captive, we have a picture of Jesus as the conquering General leading the defeated enemy in parade – disarmed, stripped, chained, totally humiliated in plain view before all of the angels of heaven. Satan and every demon were totally defeated and in their total disgrace were made a public spectacle.

When Jesus stripped the keys of authority away from Satan, He took back the keys of authority which Adam in his disobedience had surrendered to Satan. As Jesus snatched those keys of authority out of Satan's hand, He disarmed Satan of his authority over mankind and this earth. Jesus had personally defeated Satan and every one of his demons.

Received with Joy

Certainly there are no words to describe the joy of the heavenly hosts at the return of God's Son to His rightful place in heaven.

How could man describe that victorious return?

David was inspired to give us a description of this time.

Psalms 24:7-10 Lift up your heads, O you gates! And be lifted up, you everlasting doors! And the King of glory shall come in.

Who is this King of glory? The Lord strong and mighty, The Lord mighty in battle.

Lift up your heads, O you gates! And lift them up, you everlasting doors! And the King of glory shall come in.

Who is this King of glory? The Lord of hosts, He is the King of glory. Selah

Proclaimed Victory!

The apostle John gives us Jesus' words, as He proclaimed His victory!

Revelation 1:18 I am He who lives, and was dead, and behold, I am alive forevermore. Amen. And I have the keys of Hades and of Death.

JESUS HAD THE KEYS!

Jesus came into heaven shouting, "Father, I have the keys! Satan is defeated and I have the keys!"

Jesus had the keys of authority in His hand which He had taken away from Satan who had stolen them in the garden when he had deceived Adam and Eve.

Importance of Keys

Jesus had taken the keys back from Satan, but He did not keep them. He gave them back to mankind.

In the first revelation of the church, Jesus told the disciples that He would give them the keys of the kingdom of heaven.

Matthew 16:19 And I will give you the keys of the kingdom of heaven, and whatever you bind on earth will be bound in heaven, and whatever you loose on earth will be loosed in heaven.

In Isaiah there is another reference to keys.

Isaiah 22:22 The key of the house of David I will lay on his shoulder; so he shall open, and no one shall shut; and he shall shut, and no one shall open.

In the past, keys were very large, heavy and ornate. The wealthy men often carried them on their shoulders because of their weight, but more due to their beauty. Often two or three slaves would follow the wealthy man carrying the keys on their shoulders. This was a show of wealth.

When Isaiah prophesied of the coming of the Messiah, he referred to the significance of the keys being carried on the shoulders.

Isaiah 9:6a For unto us a Child is born, unto us a Son is given; and the government will be upon His shoulder.

The keys, the government and the authority, were in Jesus' hands! Jesus took those keys and gave them to His church.

The authority on this earth has been restored to mankind!

QUESTIONS FOR REVIEW

1. After His death on the cross, where did Jesus take all of our sins and iniquities?

2. What does the Scripture mean when it says that Jesus spoiled principalities and powers and put them to an open shame?

3. What is represented by the keys that Jesus mentioned in Revelation 1:18?

Lesson Seven

Authority Restored to Mankind

WORK OF JESUS COMPLETE!

The work of Jesus was, and is, complete!

When God created Adam and Eve, He gave them the authority to rule this earth. Through sin, they lost this authority to Satan. Then Jesus, the perfect man, the Last Adam, walked on this earth in every manner that God had created man to do. Jesus had taken the sins of all mankind on Himself and died on the cross paying the penalty for that sin.

He had suffered death for all mankind. He had delivered those sins to the depths of the pit and then the power of God Himself had come on Jesus. He defeated Satan and all the demons at the gates of hell. Jesus took back the keys of authority.

Jesus took back everything Satan had stolen from mankind. Everything God had created Adam and Eve to be and to have had been reclaimed and given back to mankind by Jesus.

When Jesus first spoke of the church that He would build, He said,

Matthew 16:18b,19 On this rock I will build my church, the gates of Hades shall not prevail against it. And I will give you the keys of the kingdom of heaven, and whatever you bind on earth will be bound in heaven, and whatever you loose on earth will be loosed in heaven.

Jesus in Heaven

The writer of the book of Hebrews gives us the position of Jesus today.

Hebrews 10:12,13 But this Man, after He had offered one sacrifice for sins forever, sat down at the right hand of God, from that time waiting till His enemies are made His footstool.

Jesus is seated at the right hand of the Father.

David also foretold the present day position of Jesus.

Psalm 110:1 The Lord said to my Lord, "Sit at My right hand, Till I make Your enemies Your footstool."

David prophesied that Jesus would be seated at the right hand of the Father.

Jesus Is Waiting

Both David and the writer of the book of Hebrews told us that Jesus is doing more than sitting at the right hand of the Father. Jesus is waiting for His enemies to be made His footstool.

Who is going to make His enemies His footstool?

Jesus is waiting for the redeemed of the Lord to discover their restored authority and to demonstrate that Satan is a defeated foe. The work of Jesus is complete! He is waiting for His enemies to be made His footstool. It is the work of the believers to put Satan in his place. The believers must put Satan and his demons under the feet of Jesus.

Jesus has done everything He was supposed to do. Now the responsibility is ours. We are His body on this earth. We are His hands, His legs, His feet. We are the ones that are to rule our world today.

PRAYER OF PAUL

The apostle Paul prayed an important, powerful prayer for all the saints. His prayer covered the position of Jesus at the right hand of the Father, our position, our power and our responsibilities.

Ephesians 1:18-23 ... the eyes of your understanding being enlightened; that you may know what is the hope of His calling, what are the riches of the glory of His inheritance in the saints, and what is the exceeding greatness of His power toward us who believe, according to the working of His mighty power which He worked in Christ when He raised Him from the dead and seated Him at His right hand in the heavenly places, far above all principality and power and might and dominion, and every name that is named, not only in this age but also in that which is to come.

And He put all things under His feet, and gave Him to be head over all things to the church, which is His body, the fullness of Him who fills all in all.

Position of Jesus

According to the apostle Paul,
- ➤ Jesus is raised from the dead
- ➤ Seated at right hand in heavenly realms
- ➤ Far above all rule, authority, power, dominion
- ➤ Above every title that can be given

➤ All things are under His feet

➤ Appointed to be the head

Jesus is far above all demonic powers. Jesus is far above every title that can be given, or will ever be given. All things are under the feet of Jesus.

Standard of Power

There are two standards of power. One in the Old Testament and another in the New Testament.

In the Old Testament the standard of power was the parting of the Red Sea.

In the New Testament the standard of power was and still is, the power of the resurrection of Jesus Christ.

Paul wrote,

Ephesians 1:19b,20a According to the working of His mighty power which He worked in Christ when He raised Him from the dead ...

Position of Believers

The apostle Paul prayed that believers would be enlightened; that they would know:

➤ The hope of His calling

➤ The riches of the glory of His inheritance

➤ Exceeding greatness of His power

➤ We are His body

➤ We are the fullness of Him

We are to have a knowledge of the riches of the glory of His inheritance and of His incomparable great power for us who believe. We are to operate in the same great power that raised Jesus from the dead!

FULLNESS OF HIM

Paul prayed for "the church, which is his body, the fullness of him who fills all in all."

If we, His church, are fulfilling a void or emptiness in the Son of God, when did this emptiness occur? Perhaps this emptiness goes back to the time Lucifer, the anointed cherub who covers, was cast out of heaven with the angels who followed him in his rebellion.

Ezekiel 28:14 You were the anointed cherub who covers; I established you; you were on the holy mountain of God; you walked back and forth in the midst of fiery stones.

Angelic Leadership

As there is a trinity in the Godhead, there also appeared to be a trinity in the leadership of the angels. There were Michael, Lucifer and Gabriel.

➤ *One-Third*

When Lucifer rebelled, it was said that "his angels" were cast out with him.

Revelation 12:7-9 And war broke out in heaven: Michael and his angels fought against the dragon; and the dragon and his angels fought, but they did not prevail, nor was a place found for them in heaven any longer.

So the great dragon was cast out, that serpent of old, called the Devil and Satan, who deceives the whole world; he was cast to the earth, and his angels were cast out with him.

The angels that were described as Satan's angels and were cast down to the earth with him, comprised one-third of all the angels of heaven.

Revelation 12:4a His tail drew a third of the stars of heaven and threw them to the earth.

➤ *Michael*

Michael was the only one referred to as an archangel.

Jude 1:9a Yet Michael the archangel ...

It was Michael and "his angels" that were the warrior angels which fought against Satan, "the dragon and his angels."

Revelation 12:7 And war broke out in heaven: Michael and his angels fought against the dragon; and the dragon and his angels fought ...

Perhaps as the archangel, Michael and a third of the angels under his command, minister to the Father.

➤ *Gabriel*

Perhaps Gabriel, who always appears as the messenger angel, and a third of the angels under his command, minister to the Holy Spirit.

He appeared to Zechariah, to give him the message that his wife Elizabeth would bear a son who would be "filled with the Holy Spirit even from birth."

Luke 1:19 And the angel answered and said to him, "I am Gabriel, who stands in the presence of God, and was sent to speak to you and bring you these glad tidings."

Gabriel also appeared to a virgin named Mary.

Luke 1:30,31,35 Then the angel said to her, "Do not be afraid, Mary, for you have found favor with God. And behold, you will conceive in your womb and bring forth a Son, and shall call His name Jesus."

Mary asked, "How can this be ... since I do not know a man?"

And the angel answered and said to her, "The Holy Spirit will come upon you, and the power of the Highest will overshadow you; therefore, also, that Holy One who is to be born will be called the Son of God."

Gabriel revealed the work of the Holy Spirit.

➤ *Lucifer*

Could it be then, that Lucifer and his angels ministered to the Son of God?

Lucifer ministered as the covering cherub, and he was depicted by the covering cherubs who were on each side of the Mercy Seat. He was right beside the throne of God. As we have seen, the covering was a ministry of praise and worship.

When, suddenly in his rebellion, Lucifer and all of his angels were cast out of heaven, how was this void to be filled?

Did the Father ask Michael and Gabriel to reassign some of their angels to fill this void in ministering to the Son? We have no record of that happening.

Could it be that God had a better plan when He created mankind in His image, to be worshipers of Him, to be seated with Him in heavenly places, to be at His side and to rule and reign with Him through all eternity?

Void Is Filled

Men and women, created in God's image, can only be complete and fulfilled as the Creator once again breathes Himself into them at the moment of salvation. He fills the emptiness in lives with Himself. Now His body is to fulfill the emptiness in Him by giving themselves to Him in a ministry of praise and worship.

In the beginning, there was only one ministry, the ministry of praise and worship. When that ceased, many other ministries became necessary – the ministries of healing, deliverance, reconciliation, restoration and others.

Could it be that as the ministry of praise and worship is restored to the church, these other ministries will no longer be as necessary within the body of Christ as they are today?

As we spend more and more time ministering in praise and worship of God, we will discover that there is a decreasing need for healing or deliverance or other ministries in our lives.

We are important to God! We are to be fulfilling to Him. We are to minister to Him in praise and worship. By so doing, we as His body become the "fullness of Him who fills all in all."

Ephesians 1:22,23 And He put all things under His feet, and gave Him to be head over all things to the church, which is His body, the fullness of Him who fills all in all.

As we praise and worship God, we are not only fulfilling the former function of Lucifer and his angels, we are demonstrating the fact that they are defeated and have no more place in heaven. We are humiliating them and putting them under our feet. As we dance before the Lord, we are crushing Satan into defeat by the very action of our feet.

> **Note:** For an in-depth study of praise and worship, read the Praise And Worship Manual by A.L. and Joyce Gill.

WHAT THIS MEANS TO US

By the work of Jesus on the cross and by the events that followed, Satan has been defeated! Every demon has been defeated! Jesus defeated them and brought them to nothing! He made a big "zero" out of them.

➤ Why are we letting Satan defeat us now?

➤ Why are we letting him take our homes from us, our cities, our nations?

➤ Why are we letting him put disease on us?

➤ Why are we accepting poverty?

The answer is that we must study and know what we have been given in Jesus Christ. We must discover our restored authority.

We Are Delivered!

When the apostle Paul wrote to the Colossians, he said we have been:

➤ Delivered

➤ Translated

➤ Redeemed

➤ Forgiven

Colossians 1:13,14 He has delivered us from the power of darkness and translated us into the kingdom of the Son of His love, in whom we have redemption through His blood, the forgiveness of sins.

Kingdom Is Here

What is the kingdom of the Son?

When Jesus taught the disciples to pray, He prayed these words:

Matthew 6:10 Your kingdom come. Your will be done on earth as it is in heaven.

The kingdom of God is not something out in the future. It is here now. We have been delivered from the dominion of darkness and brought into the kingdom of the Son through redemption and the forgiveness of our sins.

With the knowledge of our restored authority, we can become forceful men and women who will have an important part in forcefully advancing the kingdom of heaven on this earth.

Matthew 11:12 And from the days of John the Baptist until now the kingdom of heaven suffers violence, and the violent take it by force.

Paul continued with a wonderful description of Jesus.

Colossians 1:15-18 He is the image of the invisible God, the firstborn over all creation. For by Him all things were created that are in heaven and that are on earth, visible and invisible, whether thrones or dominions or principalities or powers. All things were created through Him and for Him. And He is before all things, and in Him all things consist. And He is the head of the body, the church, who is the beginning, the firstborn from the dead, that in all things He may have the preeminence.

Jesus our Head

Jesus:
➢ **Is the image of God**
➢ **Creator of all things**
➢ **Was before all things**
➢ **Holds all things together**
➢ **Is the head of the body, the church**
➢ **Is the beginning, firstborn from among the dead.**

Jesus is our head. We are His body. His body is made up of all believers. As His body, we are described as having already been rescued from Satan's dominion and translated into a brand new kingdom where we will reign in dominion with Jesus, the Son of God. We are described as being redeemed and completely forgiven from all sins.

The head of the body, Jesus, is in heaven. The rest of His body, including His feet, is on earth. It is on earth that man must fulfill his function of absolute dominion. It is here that we must forcibly advance the kingdom of God by effective spiritual warfare.

SATAN'S POSITION

Under Jesus' Feet

God placed Satan under Jesus' feet and appointed Jesus to be the head over everything concerning the church.

Ephesians 1:22 And He put all things under His feet, and gave Him to be head over all things to the church.

Under our Feet

Romans 16:20a And the God of peace will crush Satan under your feet shortly.

To be under one's feet is a picture of being totally conquered, defeated and subdued. It is a picture of absolute authority and dominion.

Genesis 3:15 And I will put enmity between you and the woman, and between your seed and her Seed; He shall bruise your head, and you shall bruise His heel.

Under our Authority

Satan is under Jesus' feet because Jesus completely defeated him and ascended far above him and all of his demons. Satan and his demons are now to be put under our feet as we discover our restored authority and begin to use that authority on earth.

Trampled Upon

Luke gives us a clear picture of Satan's position. He is to be trampled under our feet. We are also promised that nothing shall in any way hurt us.

Luke 10:19 (Amplified) Behold! I have given you authority and power to trample upon serpents and scorpions, and (physical and mental strength and ability) over all the power that the enemy [possesses], and nothing shall in any way harm you.

Mankind having been rescued, brought in, redeemed, forgiven and completely restored to God's image on earth, is now to trample Satan under his feet and demonstrate that he is a defeated enemy.

When Isaiah described the end of Satan, he referred to his being as one trampled underfoot.

Isaiah 14:18-20 All the kings of the nations, all of them, sleep in glory, everyone in his own house; but you are cast out of your grave like an abominable branch, Like the garment of those who are slain, thrust through with a sword, who go down to the stones of the pit, like a corpse trodden under foot.

You will not be joined with them in burial, because you have destroyed your land and slain your people. The brood of evildoers shall never be named.

CHAIN OF COMMAND

When Jesus ascended back to His Father, He laid aside His rights as the Son of Man and took back upon Himself all of His rights as the Son of God.

Man's Rights on Earth

As God, He no longer exercises dominion on earth because, here, He gave all dominion to man.

It is man who must put Satan under his feet on the earth as he was created to do.

The prophet Isaiah gave us a wonderful, encouraging prophecy.

➤ In righteousness you will be established
➤ Oppression will be far from you
➤ You have nothing to fear
➤ Terror will not come near you
➤ If anyone attacks you, they will surrender
➤ No weapon formed against you will prosper
➤ You will refute every tongue that comes against you

Isaiah 54:14-17 "In righteousness you shall be established; you shall be far from oppression, for you shall not fear; and from terror, for it shall not come near you.

"Indeed they shall surely assemble, but not because of Me. Whoever assembles against you shall fall for your sake.

"Behold, I have created the blacksmith who blows the coals in the fire, who brings forth an instrument for his work; and I have created the spoiler to destroy. No weapon formed against you shall prosper, and every tongue which rises against you in judgment you shall condemn. This is the heritage of the servants of the Lord, and their righteousness is from Me," says the Lord.

Our heritage is something that belongs to us by right of birth.

Isaiah prophesied,
This is the heritage of the servants of the Lord!

QUESTIONS FOR REVIEW

1. If all things are under the feet of Jesus, why are the devil and demon powers still able to continue their evil work on this earth?

2. Why is God allowing Satan to continue his evil on earth after Jesus has defeated Him by His death on the cross and by His resurrection?

3. What changes are necessary in your life if you are to walk in your restored authority – to demonstrate that Satan is a defeated enemy?

Satan's Strategies Today

WHAT HAPPENED?

2,000 YEARS LATER – SATAN HAS ASSUMED THAT AUTHORITY

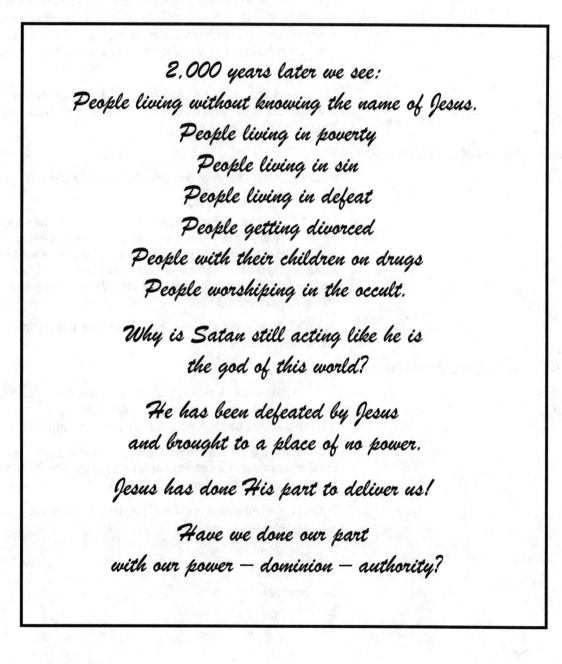

2,000 years later we see:

People living without knowing the name of Jesus.

People living in poverty

People living in sin

People living in defeat

People getting divorced

People with their children on drugs

People worshiping in the occult.

Why is Satan still acting like he is
the god of this world?

He has been defeated by Jesus
and brought to a place of no power.

Jesus has done His part to deliver us!

Have we done our part
with our power – dominion – authority?

SATAN'S STRATEGIES

To Steal, Kill and Destroy

Through all the ages, Satan's intent has not changed.

John 10:10a The thief does not come except to steal, and to kill, and to destroy.

The devil hates us so much that he has given orders through the ranks of his demonic army to steal, kill and destroy! Assignments have been issued to rob us of necessities for our lives and ministries. Orders have been issued to kill us through spirits of infirmity, murder and suicide. Tragic accidents are to be attempted on our lives. The devil has issued his decree, "Whatever it takes, they must be destroyed!"

If demons are unable to kill us, perhaps, they can report that they have slowed us down or stopped us from fulfilling our God-given ministries.

Assign Spirits of Infirmity

Satan attempts to steal our health by using demon spirits of infirmity.

Luke 13:11-13 And behold, there was a woman who had a spirit of infirmity eighteen years, and was bent over and could in no way raise herself up. But when Jesus saw her, He called her to Him and said to her, "Woman, you are loosed from your infirmity." And He laid His hands on her, and immediately she was made straight, and glorified God.

John 5:5 Now a certain man was there who had an infirmity thirty-eight years.

To Press, Perplex, Persecute

The apostle Paul describes Satan's attack on his life and ministry. It is encouraging to see that all of Satan's attempts failed to stop Paul's ministry for the Lord.

2 Corinthians 4:8,9 We are hard pressed on every side, yet not crushed; we are perplexed, but not in despair; persecuted, but not forsaken; struck down, but not destroyed.

Satan attacks all that is good and positive in our lives:
➢ Marriages
➢ Children
➢ Families
➢ Friends
➢ Ministries

> Health
> Joy
> Peace

OUR DEFENSE

Know Enemy's Strategy

Men and women perish for lack of knowledge. If they are going to stop Satan from his goal of stealing, killing and destroying, they must know the enemy and his strategy.

> Satan brings death – God brings life.
> Satan brings hate – God brings love.

Jesus

> *Destroyed Death*

Jesus has destroyed death and brought life and immortality.

2 Timothy 1:10 ... but has now been revealed by the appearing of our Savior Jesus Christ, who has abolished death and brought life and immortality to light through the gospel.

> *Destroyed Devil's Power*

Jesus has destroyed the devil and freed us from the fear of death.

Hebrews 2:14,15 Inasmuch then as the children have partaken of flesh and blood, He Himself likewise shared in the same, that through death He might destroy him who had the power of death, that is, the devil, and release those who through fear of death were all their lifetime subject to bondage.

> *Delivered from Slavery*

Satan has no right to hold us in slavery. We, through faith in Jesus Christ, have been redeemed from the bondage of slavery to Satan and his kingdom.

When Satan or his demons come to steal, kill and destroy, they must not find us vulnerable, unprotected or defenseless. Instead through a knowledge of God's Word, we must be found covered with the blood of Jesus. We must stand firm with our shield of faith. We must boldly and fearlessly speak God's Word along with the prophet Isaiah.

Isaiah 54:17a No weapon formed against you shall prosper ...

SATAN'S TOP PRIORITY – ROBBING US OF GOD'S WORD

Sharpen Your Sword

If we do not have the Word in our minds and our spirits, we cannot defeat Satan and his followers with the Word. Jesus wants us to have abundance in all walks of our life. If we do not have this, we have been robbed by Satan.

We must know who we are in Christ to realize that we have already won the war!

Parable of Farmer – A Revelation for Victory

The Parable *Mark 4:3-8*	*Jesus Explained Parable* *Mark 4:14-20*
Listen! Behold, a sower went out to sow.	The sower sows the word.
And it happened, as he sowed, that some seed fell by the wayside; and the birds of the air came and devoured it.	And these are the ones by the wayside where the word is sown. And when they hear, Satan comes immediately and takes away the word that was sown in their hearts.
Some fell on stony ground, where it did not have much earth; and immediately it sprang up because it had no depth of earth. But when the sun was up it was scorched, and because it had no root it withered away.	These likewise are the ones sown on stony ground who, when they hear the word, immediately receive it with gladness; and they have no root in themselves, and so endure only for a time. Afterward, when tribulation or persecution arises for the word's sake, immediately they stumble.
And some fell among thorns; and the thorns grew up and choked it, and it yielded no crop.	Now these are the ones sown among thorns; they are the ones who hear the word, and the cares of this world, the deceitfulness of riches, and the desires for other things entering in choke the word, and it become unfruitful.
But other seed fell on good ground and yielded a crop that sprang up, increased and produced: some thirtyfold, some sixty, and some a hundred.	But these are the ones sown on good ground, those who hear the word, accept it, and bear fruit; some thirtyfold, some sixty, and some a hundred.

Many have understood this parable to refer to the seed of salvation being sown and the different results of evangelism and this is true.

However, Jesus said that He was talking about the Word of God. Jesus taught that when we receive a new understanding of God's Word, Satan would come immediately to steal it from us. This could be God's Word as it applies to any area of our lives.

How many times have you heard people say that after a close time with the Lord the trials always come? After a wonderful conference or seminar, everything seems to "fall apart." Jesus said this is Satan coming to steal the Word.

One of Three Things

When the Word is sown there are three things that can happen:

➤ Satan may steal the Word immediately if we become offended when Satan brings tribulation and persecution.

➤ The Word may be strangled by the worries of this life, the deceitfulness of wealth or by sinful desires.

➤ The Word can be allowed to take root and spring up.

Tribulation / Persecution

Jesus warned them that tribulation and persecution would arise for the Word's sake.

Mark 4:17 ... and they have no root in themselves, and so endure only for a time. Afterward, when tribulation or persecution arises for the word's sake, immediately they stumble.

Satan Comes Immediately

Satan knows that if the revelation of God's Word is allowed to remain in our hearts, by that same Word, he can be defeated. While he has many plans and strategies to bring defeat into our lives, his top priority is always to rob us of the revelation of the Word of God. Jesus said Satan always comes when they hear.

Mark 4:15 And these are the ones by the wayside where the word is sown. And when they hear, Satan comes immediately and takes away the word that was sown in their hearts.

JESUS CALMED THE SEA

When Jesus finished teaching, He and the disciples went out in the boat. Soon Jesus was asleep in the back. Then Satan came with the worries of this life.

Mark 4:35-41 On the same day, when evening had come, He said to them, "Let us cross over to the other side."

Now when they had left the multitude, they took Him along in the boat as He was. And other little boats were also with Him. And a great windstorm arose, and the waves beat into the boat, so that it was already filling. But He was in the stern, asleep on a pillow. And they awoke Him and said to Him, "Teacher, do You not care that we are perishing?"

Then He arose and rebuked the wind, and said to the sea, "Peace, be still!" And the wind ceased and there was a great calm. But He said to them, "Why are you so fearful? How is it that you have no faith?"

And they feared exceedingly, and said to one another, "Who can this be, that even the wind and the sea obey Him!"

The storm which came up was one of the tribulations or persecutions Jesus had said Satan would bring as soon as the Word was sown.

Notice the disciples' reaction. They were offended. "Teacher, do You not care that we are perishing?" They were offended because Jesus was sleeping and not afraid as they were, and they accused Him of not caring.

We Have a Choice

When Satan brings tribulation and persecution against us in an attempt to rob us of the Word of God, we have a choice. We can thank the Lord for warning us so that we are not ignorant of Satan's schemes and then rebuke him. We can become offended, lose our joy and thereby allow Satan to rob from us the revelation of God's Word which has been sown into our hearts.

How often when the tribulation and persecutions come, have we begun to cry out and blame God?

➤ "Teacher, don't you care that we're going to drown?

➤ "God, Don't you care my children are going astray?

➤ "God, don't you care that sickness has come against my life?

➤ "God, don't you care that I can't pay my bills?"

When we allow ourselves to become offended and blame God for the storms in our life, we are allowing Satan to rob us of the precious seed of God's Word.

Speaking by Faith

A positive action of faith is necessary if we are going to keep the seed of the Word in our hearts and expect a great harvest of thirty, sixty or even a hundred times what was sown.

Mark 4:40 But He said to them, "Why are you so fearful? How is it that you have no faith?"

Speaking with Authority

Instead of becoming offended when the storms of life come against our boat, we must stand up against the devil and boldly speak the Word of God in faith.

Mark 4:39 Then He arose and rebuked the wind, and said to the sea, "Peace, be still!" And the wind ceased and there was a great calm.

Be Alert

Even though Satan is a defeated foe, he will do every thing to keep us from walking in our God-given authority. We must be alert, on guard and ready to overcome every attack against our lives

1 Peter 5:8 Be sober, be vigilant; because your adversary the devil walks about like a roaring lion, seeking whom he may devour.

God's Armor

By faith, we are to put on God's armor so that we can stand against the devil's schemes.

Ephesians 6:10,11 Finally, my brethren, be strong in the Lord and in the power of His might. Put on the whole armor of God, that you may be able to stand against the wiles of the devil.

When we do this, we will find ourselves standing up to the devil in the middle of the storm.

Ephesians 6:13 Therefore take up the whole armor of God, that you may be able to withstand in the evil day, and having done all, to stand.

Our Authority

Jesus' work is complete! He has already defeated the devil and his demons.

On earth, He has created men and women to walk in authority. He has restored our authority, and now, we must rise up and demonstrate that the devil is a defeated foe. We must forcibly advance the kingdom of God on this earth.

QUESTIONS FOR REVIEW

1. According to John 10:10, Satan comes to attack our lives with three primary objectives. Name these three objectives.

2. According to the parable of the farmer what is Satan's top priority as a thief?

3. Why is it important that we act in authority and not allow ourselves to become angry when we face tribulation and persecution?

Lesson Nine

The Church and Authority

WHAT IS THE CHURCH?

First Mention

Throughout the Old Testament, worship had always centered around the tabernacle, the temple, or a synagogue. There was no church as we know it today.

When Jesus first mentioned the church, He also revealed the three things which were to characterize it above all its other functions. It would be built by Jesus. It was to be a victorious overcoming army which would prevail against the gates of hell. It would have the power to bind and loose.

Matthew 16:13-18 When Jesus came into the region of Caesarea Philippi, He asked His disciples, saying, "Who do men say that I, the Son of Man, am?"

So they said, "Some say John the Baptist, some Elijah, and others Jeremiah or one of the prophets."

He said to them, "But who do you say that I am?"

And Simon Peter answered and said, "You are the Christ, the Son of the living God."

Jesus answered and said to him, "Blessed are you, Simon Bar-Jonah, for flesh and blood has not revealed this to you, but My Father who is in heaven.

"And I also say to you that you are Peter, and on this rock I will build My church, and the gates of Hades shall not prevail against it."

Foundational Truth

Peter knew by a revelation from God that Jesus was the Christ, the Son of God. This was the truth upon which the church was to be built.

Built by Jesus

The first characteristic of the church is that Jesus would build it. It would not be built by men, by men's traditions or programs.

Overcomes Gates of Hell

The second characteristic is that the gates of hell will not overcome it.

In the Amplified Bible we read,
I will build my church, and the gates of Hades (the powers of the infernal region) shall not overpower it – or be strong to its detriment, or hold out against it.

Keys to Bind and Loose

The church has the power to bind and loose.

Matthew 16:19 And I will give you the keys of the kingdom of heaven, and whatever you bind on earth will be bound in heaven, and whatever you loose on earth will be loosed in heaven.

There are three things which we need to learn about the church from this first time Jesus mentioned it.

➢ The church would be built by Jesus on the revelation from the Father that Jesus is the Christ, the Son of the living God.

➢ The gates of Hades would not be able to hold out against the church.

➢ The church would be given the keys of the kingdom of heaven and have the power of binding and loosing.

THE KEYS RESTORED

We have established that the keys refer to the authority on this earth. The keys can either lock or unlock the gates which we have seen are the governments over any entity whether it be a person, a family, an organization, a city, a state or a nation.

Keys to Rule

These were the keys of authority which God gave to mankind when He created man and woman in His own image.

Genesis 1:26 Then God said, "Let Us make man in Our image, according to Our likeness; let them have dominion over the fish of the sea, over the birds of the air, and over the cattle, over all the earth and over every creeping thing that creeps on the earth."

Stolen by Satan

These keys were intended by God to be used for good on this earth. However, when Adam and Eve sinned, they surrendered the keys to Satan who had come to steal, kill and destroy.

The keys of authority, under the control of Satan became the keys of death and Hades.

Revelation 1:18 I am He who lives, and was dead, and behold, I am alive forevermore. Amen. And I have the keys of Hades and of Death.

Regained by Jesus

These were the keys of authority which Jesus snatched away from the devil after He had delivered our sins to the depths of Hades. When Jesus came smashing victoriously through the gates of Hades, He took these keys of authority away from Satan. Satan, no longer has any legal authority on this earth.

Restored to Man

These keys were the authority which Jesus restored to mankind as a new creation after His resurrection and ascension to the Father. Since these keys were restored to their original owners on this earth, they were no longer to be misused as the keys of death and Hades. Instead they became known as the keys of the kingdom of heaven.

Keys of Kingdom

Matthew 16:19 And I will give you the keys of the kingdom of heaven, and whatever you bind on earth will be bound in heaven, and whatever you loose on earth will be loosed in heaven.

With these keys we can establish God's will and God's kingdom on earth.

This is the victory for which Jesus taught His disciples to pray.

Matthew 6:9,10 In this manner, therefore, pray: Our Father in heaven, hallowed be Your name. Your kingdom come. Your will be done on earth as it is in heaven.

As we, the body of Christ, use our God-given keys of authority according to His will, we are establishing the Kingdom of Heaven on this earth.

THE GATES OF HELL

Church on the Offensive

When Jesus first mentioned the word, church, He immediately stated that the gates of hell will not prevail against it.

Matthew 16:18b ... My church, and the gates of Hades shall not prevail against it.

It is important to understand what Jesus meant when He said the gates of Hades would not overcome the church.

In our time, we think of a gate as an opening in a fence, or wall. With that picture in our mind, it is hard to gain any real understanding of this verse. Most of us have never been attacked by a gate.

What Are the Gates?

In biblical times, the government and business of a city was conducted at its gates. Therefore, the gates while providing security to a walled city, also became a reference to a city's or a nation's government. King Solomon referred to this in one of his proverbs.

Proverbs 31:23 Her husband is known in the gates, when he sits among the elders of the land.

To Possess the Gates

When God blessed Abraham, he referred to possessing the gates of his enemies. That was a blessing.

Genesis 22:17 In blessing I will bless you, and in multiplying I will multiply your descendants as the stars of the heaven and as the sand which is on the seashore; and your descendants shall possess the gate of their enemies.

The blessing placed upon Rebekah also referred to possessing the gates of the enemies.

Genesis 24:60 And they blessed Rebekah and said to her: "Our sister, may you become the mother of thousands of ten thousands; and may your descendants possess the gates of those who hate them."

To possess the gates of the enemy means to take over and control its government. Today we are to possess the gates of our enemies in the spirit realm. By authority, dominion and aggressive, violent spiritual warfare the gates are taken by force.

King Solomon spoke of this.

Proverbs 14:19 The evil will bow before the good, and the wicked at the gates of the righteous.

Many have pictured themselves being attacked by the devil while they cower inside the gates in anxious fear. However, it is the church and not Satan who is to be on the offense.

We, the church, are to be storming the gates of hell and forcibly advancing the kingdom of God throughout the world.

KEYS TO THE KINGDOM

When Jesus first mentioned the church, He said, "I will give you the keys." That was to happen in the future. Later, after His death and resurrection, He told the Father, "I have the keys!"

The keys represent man's restored authority. It was these keys which Jesus snatched away from Satan when He disarmed powers and authorities.

What is this kingdom of heaven to which we hold the keys?

Jesus, the King of Kings, reigns with the Father over all the universe. It is on planet earth that His kingdom is to be established.

The kingdom of God will be forcibly advanced throughout the world as redeemed men and women use their restored keys of spiritual authority.

These are the keys Jesus said we would use to bind and loose. We have the authority to bind Satan and his demons and we have the keys of authority to loose the captives! When we win the battle in the realm of the spirit it will be manifest in the natural, or fleshly realm.

PRINCIPLE OF BINDING AND LOOSING

Jesus said He would give us the keys of the kingdom of heaven and whatever we bound on earth would be bound in heaven and whatever we loosed on earth would be loosed in heaven.

What does that mean?

Jesus Bound Strong Man

Jesus talked about binding the strong man.

Matthew 12:28,29 But if I cast out demons by the Spirit of God, surely the kingdom of God has come upon you. Or else how can one enter a strong man's house and plunder his goods, unless he first binds the strong man? And then he will plunder his house.

Who Is Strong Man?

The strong man is Satan or the ruling demon which he has assigned over a government, an organization, or over a person's life.

Jesus entered the strong man's house and bound the strong man (Satan and his ruling demons).

We bind Satan and then his ruling demons by saying with authority,

➢ "Satan, I bind you in the name of Jesus!"

Next we are to bind the strong man, by boldly saying to that demon ruler,

➢ "You foul demon spirit, I bind you in the name of Jesus!"

What Is Binding?

To bind means to limit Satan or a demon ruler over a particular situation where God has led us into spiritual warfare.

As an example, when we tie a dog with a chain that is fastened to a stake, the dog can only go a certain distance. He is limited from reaching beyond the length of the chain into the area from which we have bound him. We have limited his realm of influence. This is what the word, bind, means.

Spoil his House

Next, we are to spoil his house. We do this by commanding the demons under the strong man's authority to,

➢ "Get out in the name of Jesus!"

We can know the identity of these spirits by the operation in the spiritual gifts of the discerning of spirits and the word of knowledge. We can also know their identity by their obvious functions.

Some of these are:
➢ Occult spirits,
➢ Hindering spirits,
➢ Unclean spirits – lustful, perverted spirits,
➢ Spirits of infirmity,
➢ Tormenting spirits,
➢ Spirits of suicide

Cast out Spirits!

By casting out these spirits we are spoiling the strong man's house. When his house is spoiled, he becomes helpless and we can command him to leave in the name of Jesus.

Luke 11:21,22 When a strong man, fully armed, guards his own palace, his goods are in peace. But when a stronger than he comes

upon him and overcomes him, he takes from him all his armor in which he trusted, and divides his spoils.

Jesus has already disarmed the powers and authorities and made a public spectacle of them. He has ascended far above all of them and is seated on the right hand of the Father. This is an accomplished fact in heaven.

Believer's Authority

As believers, we must exercise our authority and dominion on earth. We must now accomplish and enforce on earth what has already been accomplished in the rest of the universe – what is an established fact in heaven. On earth, we must bind Satan and his ruling demons and loose the captives. We must limit his realm of influence.

Matthew 16:19b Whatever you bind on earth will be bound in heaven, and whatever you loose on earth will be loosed in heaven.

As we do this we, too, are disarming the powers and authorities and making a public spectacle of them, triumphing over them by the cross.

SATAN'S POSITION

Made of No Effect

Jesus by His death and resurrection, made Satan of no effect.

Hebrews 2:14 (Amplified Bible) Since, therefore, [these His] children share in flesh and blood – that is, in the physical nature of human beings – He [Himself] in a similar manner partook of the same [nature], that by [going through] death He might bring to naught and make of no effect him who had the power of death, that is, the devil.

No Longer our Captor

We are set free from the fear of death and bondage.

Hebrews 2:15 ... and release those who through fear of death were all their lifetime subject to bondage.

By the accomplished work of Jesus in His death and victorious resurrection, men and women need no longer be held captive to the fear of death. When we discover this truth, we are set free and completely delivered from bondage and fear of the devil.

Works Are Destroyed

Why was the Son of God manifested?
➤ **To destroy the works of Satan!**
➤ **To make a public spectacle of them!**

1 John 3:8 He who sins is of the devil, for the devil has sinned from the beginning. For this purpose the Son of God was manifested, that He might destroy the works of the devil.

Colossians 2:15 Having disarmed principalities and powers, He made a public spectacle of them, triumphing over them in it.

SLEEPING CHURCH IS AWAKENING!

When Jesus came to this earth to destroy the works of the devil, He laid aside His authority as God. On earth as the Last Adam, He walked and ministered with authority and dominion.

Satan was completely defeated by Jesus. He was brought to naught and made of no effect. Jesus made a big "zero" out of the devil.

Now this authority and dominion are the keys which have been restored to redeemed mankind who, through faith, are now His church and His body on earth.

As a defeated foe, the only thing that Satan can do on this earth is what we in our ignorance have been letting him do. With this revelation from God's Word, we can rise up and bind Satan and his ruling demons. We can pull down the strongholds of Satan when we bind the strong man and spoil his house, when we command demon spirits to flee in the name of Jesus.

2 Corinthians 10:4 For the weapons of our warfare are not carnal but mighty in God for pulling down strongholds.

The church which Jesus said He would build has been a sleeping giant. Now, it is awakening to operate in its God-given authority and it will demolish the strongholds of Satan!

QUESTIONS FOR REVIEW

1. What did Jesus mean when He said that the "gates of Hades would not overcome" the church?
2. Jesus said that we are to bind and we are to loose. Describe how you plan to carry out these important instructions from Jesus.
3. Having bound the strong man over one of Satan's strongholds, Jesus said that one is to spoil his goods. Who is it described as the strong man? What is the procedure for spoiling his goods?

The Keys to the Kingdom

JESUS HAS THE KEYS

Do you remember the triumphant words Jesus shouted as He came back into heaven?

Revelation 1:18 I am He who lives, and was dead, and behold, I am alive forevermore. Amen. And I have the keys of Hades and of Death.

Jesus took the keys of hell and death away from Satan. Once Jesus had delivered our sins to the depths of Hades, it was not possible for Him to be held captive there any longer.

Acts 2:24 ... whom God raised up, having loosed the pains of death, because it was not possible that He should be held by it.

Jesus defeated death!

Jesus restored the authority, dominion, and kingship to man. He restored to us everything that Satan had stolen.

We know that God wants us to live in total dominion and authority over Satan because He sacrificed His own Son to restore all that He had created us to be and to do on this earth.

All that Jesus did on this earth, His life, His death, and His resurrection was so that we could once again be restored. He did it so that we could walk in authority and be victorious over Satan, his demons, and all on this earth.

THE BLOOD OF JESUS – AN OVERCOMING KEY FOR VICTORY

When God created Adam, He breathed into him His own life. This life was not limited to one isolated part of Adam's body. God put His life into the blood of Adam. It was being continuously pumped to every part of Adam's body.

Moses wrote that the life of a creature was in the blood.

Leviticus 17:11a For the life of the flesh is in the blood ...

Adam's Sin – Death

Through sin, Adam lost the life of God which was in his blood. This life could only be restored to man through God's plan of redemption. For man to be restored to God's image, he must once again have the life of God in his blood.

In God's plan of redemption, His Son Jesus would shed His own blood.

Hebrews 9:22 And according to the law almost all things are purged with blood, and without shedding of blood there is no remission.

The penalty for sin, which was death, had to be paid by a perfect Substitute who had not lost the life of God in his blood through sin.

Conceived by the Holy Spirit and born of a virgin, Jesus had not inherited the blood of Adam. He became that perfect Substitute who willfully gave up His life by shedding his own innocent blood.

Through Jesus' Blood We Have

➤ *Forgiveness of Sins*

Our redemption is in the blood of Jesus.

Ephesians 1:7 In Him we have redemption through His blood, the forgiveness of sins, according to the riches of His grace ...

1 Peter 1:18,19 ... knowing that you were not redeemed with corruptible things, like silver or gold, from your aimless conduct received by tradition from your fathers, but with the precious blood of Christ, as of a lamb without blemish and without spot.

➤ *Justification*
➤ *Salvation*

We were justified and the righteousness of God was restored to our lives by the blood of Jesus.

Romans 5:8,9 But God demonstrates His own love toward us, in that while we were still sinners, Christ died for us. Much more then, having now been justified by His blood, we shall be saved from wrath through Him.

The perfect justice of God was satisfied and we were saved from God's wrath when Jesus became our Substitute and bore our penalty of death by shedding His blood on the cross.

Only by partaking of the shed blood of Jesus which has God's life in it, can we once again have God's life in us.

John 6:53 Then Jesus said to them, "Most assuredly, I say to you, unless you eat the flesh of the Son of Man and drink His blood, you have no life in you."

➤ *Fellowship*

The blood of Jesus will remove all of the effects of sin upon our lives so that once again the life of God can be restored.

1 John 1:7 But if we walk in the light as He is in the light, we have fellowship with one another, and the blood of Jesus Christ His Son cleanses us from all sin.

➤ *Redemption*

Our redemption and our total forgiveness is through His blood.

Colossians 1:13,14 He has delivered us from the power of darkness and translated us into the kingdom of the Son of His love, in whom we have redemption through His blood, the forgiveness of sins.

Without receiving the sacrifice of redemption and God's gift of salvation through the shed blood of Jesus, there is no way for man to be forgiven and restored.

Hebrews 9:22 And according to the law almost all things are purged with blood, and without shedding of blood there is no remission.

Hebrews 9:12 Not with the blood of goats and calves, but with His own blood He entered the Most Holy Place once for all, having obtained eternal redemption.

➤ *Are Without Spot*
➤ *Able to Serve*

Through the blood of Jesus, we are cleansed so that we may serve God.

Hebrews 9:14 How much more shall the blood of Christ, who through the eternal Spirit offered Himself without spot to God, purge your conscience from dead works to serve the living God?

➤ *Have Confidence*

As Adam walked in daily fellowship in the presence of God before he sinned, even so by the blood of Jesus, man, freed from all guilt and condemnation, can once again walk boldly into the presence of God.

Hebrews 10:19 Therefore, brethren, having boldness to enter the Holiest by the blood of Jesus ...

➤ *Have Peace*

Peace and reconciliation are made possible through His blood.

Colossians 1:19,20 For it pleased the Father that in Him all the fullness should dwell, and by Him to reconcile all things to Himself, by Him, whether things on earth or things in heaven, having made peace through the blood of His cross.

➤ *Restored to Original Position*

It was the blood of Jesus that overcame Satan as it redeemed and restored mankind to the life of God through the new birth.

Satan came to steal, kill and destroy man whom God had created in His exact likeness and image on this earth. Through sin, man had lost the life of God. Man was helpless in Satan's attacks upon his life. By God's plan of redemption through the shedding of the blood of His own Son, man could be completely restored to his original created position and relationship to God. By the blood of Jesus, man, once held in hopeless defeat, could once again become a victorious overcomer.

➤ *Covering of Protection*

Even as the priest in the Old Testament took the blood of the sacrificial lamb and sprinkled it on the mercy seat of God to become a covering or atonement for the sins of the people, even so today, by faith, the blood of the Lamb becomes a covering of protection for redeemed mankind.

➤ *Victory*

Through the blood of Jesus, we have victory!

As we walk in forgiveness, in obedience to God and by faith, we can boldly say:

➤ "Satan, I am covered by the blood of Jesus!"

➤ "My family and my possessions are covered by the blood of Jesus!"

➤ "Satan, you have been overcome by the blood of Jesus!"

➤ "Because of the blood of Jesus, you cannot touch me!"

Even as Jesus overcame Satan by His blood, we too can be overcomers by the blood of Jesus! By the protection of His blood, no weapon formed against us can prosper.

Revelation 12:11a And they overcame him by the blood of the Lamb and by the word of their testimony.

Satan was overcome by the blood of Jesus.

The key of the authority of the blood of Jesus has been given to each one of us who through that blood have been redeemed. With the powerful key of His blood we are overcomers and Satan will continue to be defeated in our lives.

THE WORD OF GOD – AN OVERCOMING KEY FOR VICTORY

Sword of Spirit

In Ephesians, our weapon for victory in battle is described as "the sword of the Spirit, which is the word of God" (6:17). The Word of God when spoken out of our mouths becomes a mighty weapon against which Satan has no defense. As we speak the Word of God with authority, we will overcome Satan in our lives.

Revelation 12:11a And they overcame him by the blood of the Lamb and by the word of their testimony.

Word in Testimony

The "word of their testimony" could just as accurately be translated "the Word in their testimony." Our testimony is what we speak. When we stop speaking the problem, our thoughts, or our fears, and begin to boldly speak what God's Word says about our situation then we too will become overcomers.

Word Brings Victory

In order to have God's word coming continually out of our mouths, it is necessary that we read, study, and meditate on that Word. Then it will become a deeply rooted abiding faith within our lives.

1 John 2:13,14 I write to you, fathers, because you have known Him who is from the beginning. I write to you, young men, because you have overcome the wicked one. I write to you, little children, because you have known the Father.

I have written to you, fathers, because you have known Him who is from the beginning. I have written to you, young men, because you are strong, and the word of God abides in you, and you have overcome the wicked one.

These young men were said to be strong overcomers because they had the Word of God abiding in them. As they boldly spoke that Word out of their mouths in their God-given authority and dominion they had overcome the wicked one.

Ephesians 6:17 And take the helmet of salvation, and the sword of the Spirit, which is the word of God.

The sword of the Spirit is the Word of God.

Revelation 19:13-16 He was clothed with a robe dipped in blood, and His name is called The Word of God. And the armies in heaven, clothed in fine linen, white and clean, followed Him on white horses.

Now out of His mouth goes a sharp sword, that with it He should strike the nations. And He Himself will rule them with a rod of iron. He Himself treads the winepress of the fierceness and wrath of Almighty God.

And He has on His robe and on His thigh a name written: KING OF KINGS AND LORD OF LORDS.

Speak the Word

Jesus said the greatest example of faith was a man who understood authority and knew how to exercise it by speaking the word.

Matthew 8:8-10 The centurion answered and said, "Lord, I am not worthy that You should come under my roof. But only speak a word, and my servant will be healed. For I also am a man under authority, having soldiers under me. And I say to this one, 'Go,' and he goes; and to another, 'Come,' and he comes; and to my servant, 'Do this,' and he does it."

When Jesus heard it, He marveled, and said to those who followed, "Assuredly, I say to you, I have not found such great faith, not even in Israel!"

Word to be Confirmed

The Word of God will be confirmed by signs and wonders.

Mark 16:19-20 So then, after the Lord had spoken to them, He was received up into heaven, and sat down at the right hand of God.

And they went out and preached everywhere, the Lord working with them and confirming the word through the accompanying signs. Amen.

Jesus Is Word

Jesus' very name is The Word of God.

Revelation 19:13 He was clothed with a robe dipped in blood, and His name is called The Word of God.

John 1:1 In the beginning was the Word, and the Word was with God, and the Word was God.

Word Cannot Return Void

God spoke of the power of His Word through Isaiah.

Isaiah 55:11 So shall My word be that goes forth from My mouth; it shall not return to Me void, but it shall accomplish what I please, and it shall prosper in the thing for which I sent it.

God spoke of the healing power of His Word through David.

Psalms 107:20 He sent His word and healed them, and delivered them from their destructions.

The Word that we speak with authority is effective in accomplishing the things that please God. God's Word promises us that it will prosper!

Words Create

Words have the power to create.

Hebrews 11:3 By faith we understand that the worlds were framed by the word of God, so that the things which are seen were not made of things which are visible.

Words Have Authority

Jesus spoke the Word with authority.

Luke 4:36 So they were all amazed and spoke among themselves, saying, "What a word this is! For with authority and power He commands the unclean spirits, and they come out."

Word In – Word Out!

It is good to know the Word, but until we meet our situations with the Word of God spoken out of our mouths, we will not have victory!

Jesus spoke the Word with authority and power.

The God-kind of faith:
➢ **Believes the Word,**
➢ **Speaks the Word,**
➢ **Sees the Word accomplish miracles.**

The key of the Word of God cannot fail as we continue to speak with authority and dominion.

In order for us to operate in the dominion on earth for which we were created, Jesus has given us, His church, the keys of authority for victorious spiritual warfare. As we discover these keys and how to effectively use them, we will find ourselves living in victory over the struggles of life. We will find ourselves to be what Jesus has already declared us to be:

> *We are more than conquerors,*
> *We are overcomers in His name.*

QUESTIONS FOR REVIEW

1. Explain why the blood of Jesus is so effective in overcoming the attacks of the devil or demon spirits.

2. Give an example of how speaking the Word of God has given you victory in your own life.

3. What scriptures are you going to memorize to use as weapons in your spiritual battles?

The Name of Jesus

THE NAME OF JESUS – AN OVERCOMING KEY FOR VICTORY

When we use the name of Jesus we are speaking with the authority of Jesus. When we speak in that name, it has the same effect as if Jesus were standing there speaking to the situation. He has given us the right to use His name.

Signs Follow Belief in Name

Signs are to follow those who believe in Jesus' name.

Mark 16:15-18 And He said to them, "Go into all the world and preach the gospel to every creature. He who believes and is baptized will be saved; but he who does not believe will be condemned.

"And these signs will follow those who believe: in My name they will cast out demons; they will speak with new tongues; they will take up serpents; and if they drink anything deadly, it will by no means hurt them; they will lay hands on the sick, and they will recover."

There was no punctuation in the Greek, the language in which the New Testament was originally written. The punctuation that is in our Bibles was added by the translators according to their own judgment.

Mark 16:17 reads,
And these signs will accompany those who believe ...

This passage could just as accurately be translated,
And these signs will accompany those who believe in my name...

Jesus said, it is important that we believe in His name. We must understand the authority that is ours in the name of Jesus. We must boldly release that authority in faith when we use the name of Jesus.

When we boldly speak and act on our belief in the name of Jesus, we will drive out demons. We will place our hands on sick people, and they will get well.

An Awesome Right

Prior to the completed work of Jesus on the cross, no one would even dare to speak the names of God. They were considered too Holy to be spoken aloud. They were inscribed inside the Most Holy Place, and were only known to the High Priest.

When Jesus gave believers the right to use His name, it was an awesome privilege, and should never be taken lightly.

Releases Jesus' Authority

Because Jesus was the Son of God,
➢ He had all authority in heaven.

Because Jesus was the Son of Man,
➢ He had all authority on earth.

Matthew 28:18 Then Jesus came and spoke to them, saying, "All authority has been given to Me in heaven and on earth."

When we use His name, an overwhelming authority and power is released. It is as though we are standing in His place and using His authority.

A Power of Attorney

When Jesus gave us the legal right to use His name, He placed His up-most trust in our control. In legal terms, He gave us the Power of Attorney to use His name.

In our judicial system a Power of Attorney is a legal document that gives a person the right and privilege to use another's name. When the person who has been so entrusted, signs a contract on behalf of the person and attaches a copy of the Power of Attorney to that contract, it has the same legally binding effect as if that person had signed the contract in person.

Hearing from God

When Jesus was ministering on this earth, He was acting on behalf of His Father.

John 5:19 Then Jesus answered and said to them, "Most assuredly, I say to you, the Son can do nothing of Himself, but what He sees the Father do; for whatever He does, the Son also does in like manner."

Now as we minister on earth, we are to act on behalf of the Son. We must not use the name of Jesus to accomplish our own desires without first taking time to listen and hear from God.

Using Name in Vain

To attempt to use the name of Jesus to accomplish our own desires without first discerning God's will, would be to use His name in vain.

Deuteronomy 5:11 You shall not take the name of the Lord your God in vain, for the Lord will not hold him guiltless who takes His name in vain.

Name above all Names

The name of Jesus is above every name.

Philippians 2:5-11 Let this mind be in you which was also in Christ Jesus, who, being in the form of God, did not consider it robbery to be equal with God, but made Himself of no reputation, taking the form of a servant, and coming in the likeness of men.

And being found in appearance as a man, He humbled Himself and became obedient to the point of death, even the death of the cross.

Therefore God also has highly exalted Him and given Him the name which is above every name, that at the name of Jesus every knee should bow, of those in heaven, and of those on earth, and of those under the earth, and that every tongue should confess that Jesus Christ is Lord, to the glory of God the Father.

➢ Every demon power has a name.
➢ Every person has a name.
➢ Every sickness and disease has a name.
➢ Every scheme of the devil has a name.
➢ When the name of Jesus is spoken, demon powers flee.
➢ When the name of Jesus is spoken, cancer and all other diseases have to bow.
➢ When the name of Jesus is spoken, Satan's schemes are defeated.

The name of Jesus is a name above every other name. Every knee shall bow in submission to the Lordship of Jesus when His name is spoken in faith.

Demons Submit to Name

Demons know the power of the name of Jesus, and they will submit to that name.

Luke 10:17,19 Then the seventy returned with joy, saying, "Lord, even the demons are subject to us in Your name."

"Behold, I give you the authority to trample on serpents and scorpions, and over all the power of the enemy, and nothing shall by any means hurt you."

Matthew 28:18 Then Jesus came and spoke to them, saying, "All authority has been given to Me in heaven and on earth."

All authority has been given to Jesus. By using Jesus' name we have that same authority on earth.

Believe in Name

We are commanded to believe in the name of Jesus.

I John 3:23 And this is His commandment: that we should believe on the name of His Son Jesus Christ and love one another, as He gave us commandment.

We are to believe in the name of Jesus for eternal life.

John 3:18 He who believes in Him is not condemned; but he who does not believe is condemned already, because he has not believed in the name of the only begotten Son of God.

John 20:31 But these are written that you may believe that Jesus is the Christ, the Son of God, and that believing you may have life in His name.

We can have full assurance of our salvation because we believe in His name.

1 John 5:13 These things I have written to you who believe in the name of the Son of God, that you may know that you have eternal life, and that you may continue to believe in the name of the Son of God.

Ask in His Name

We are instructed to ask in the name of Jesus.

John 14:12-14 Most assuredly, I say to you, he who believes in Me, the works that I do he will do also; and greater works than these he will do, because I go to My Father. And whatever you ask in My name, that I will do, that the Father may be glorified in the Son. If you ask anything in My name, I will do it.

As Jesus was leaving to go to the Father, He instructed His followers to use His name. He told them that what they would ask, He would do, so that the Father would be glorified in the Son.

John 15:16 You did not choose Me, but I chose you and appointed you that you should go and bear fruit, and that your fruit should remain, that whatever you ask the Father in My name He may give you.

John 16:23,24 And in that day you will ask Me nothing. Most assuredly, I say to you, whatever you ask the Father in My name He will give you. Until now you have asked nothing in My name. Ask, and you will receive, that your joy may be full.

We are instructed to ask in the name of Jesus.

Do Everything in His Name

We are to do everything in the name of Jesus. What a wonderful privilege this is!

Colossians 3:17 And whatever you do in word or deed, do all in the name of the Lord Jesus, giving thanks to God the Father through Him.

We should also consider that everything we do should be suitable to do in the name of Jesus. To do this could revolutionize our way of living.

APOSTLES USED THE NAME OF JESUS

The apostles and the early believers in the book of Acts boldly used the name of Jesus with miraculous results.

Power in His Name

Acts 3:1-10 Now Peter and John went up together to the temple at the hour of prayer, the ninth hour.

And a certain man lame from his mother's womb was carried, whom they laid daily at the gate of the temple which is called Beautiful, to ask alms from those who entered the temple; who, seeing Peter and John about to go into the temple, asked for alms.

And fixing his eyes on him, with John, Peter said, "Look at us." So he gave them his attention, expecting to receive something from them.

Then Peter said, "Silver and gold I do not have, but what I do have I give you: In the name of Jesus Christ of Nazareth, rise up and walk."

And he took him by the right hand and lifted him up, and immediately his feet and ankle bones received strength.

So he, leaping up, stood and walked and entered the temple with them–walking, leaping, and praising God. And all the people saw him walking and praising God. Then they knew that it was he who sat begging alms at the Beautiful Gate of the temple; and they were filled with wonder and amazement at what had happened to him.

Faith in His Name

Peter explained that the key to using the name of Jesus, was to release the authority of that name by faith.

Acts 3:12 So when Peter saw it, he responded to the people: "Men of Israel, why do you marvel at this? Or why look so intently at us, as though by our own power or godliness we had made this man walk?"

Acts 3:16 "And His name, through faith in His name, has made this man strong, whom you see and know. Yes, the faith which comes through Him has given him this perfect soundness in the presence of you all."

Healing in His Name

As a result of this healing Peter and John were arrested, held in jail overnight, and threatened by the religious leaders not to speak any more in the name of Jesus. Peter boldly answered their question about this healing by saying:

Acts 4:10 ..."let it be known to you all, and to all the people of Israel, that by the name of Jesus Christ of Nazareth, whom you crucified, whom God raised from the dead, by Him this man stands here before you whole."

Salvation in His Name

As a result of Peter and John using the name of Jesus in ministering healing to the crippled man, the number of believing men grew to about five thousand.

Acts 4:4 However, many of those who heard the word believed; and the number of the men came to be about five thousand.

Our precious salvation is in the powerful name of Jesus.

Acts 4:12 Nor is there salvation in any other, for there is no other name under heaven given among men by which we must be saved.

Man's Fear of His Name

Peter and John were threatened by the religious leaders not to speak in that name again.

Acts 4:17,18 "But so that it spreads no further among the people, let us severely threaten them, that from now on they speak to no man in this name." And they called them and commanded them not to speak at all nor teach in the name of Jesus.

Boldness in His Name

At that moment a spirit of boldness came upon Peter and John.

Acts 4:29,30 Now, Lord, look on their threats, and grant to Your servants that with all boldness they may speak Your word, by stretching out Your hand to heal, and that signs and wonders may be done through the name of Your holy Servant Jesus.

Philip Preached His Name

> Acts 8:12 But when they believed Philip as he preached the things concerning the kingdom of God and the name of Jesus Christ, both men and women were baptized.

Arrested Because of Name

Paul was sent to arrest those who called upon the name of Jesus.

> Acts 9:14 And here he has authority from the chief priests to bind all who call on Your name.

Chosen to Carry His Name

Paul was chosen by God to carry the name of Jesus to the world.

> Acts 9:15 But the Lord said to him, "Go, for he is a chosen vessel of Mine to bear My name before Gentiles, kings, and the children of Israel."

Preached Fearlessly in Name

> Acts 9:27 But Barnabas took him and brought him to the apostles. And he declared to them how he had seen the Lord on the road, and that He had spoken to him, and how he had preached boldly at Damascus in the name of Jesus.

Deliverance Through Name

> Acts 16:18 And this she did for many days. But Paul, greatly annoyed, turned and said to the spirit, "I command you in the name of Jesus Christ to come out of her." And he came out that very hour.

High Honor for His Name

> Acts 19:17,18 This became known both to all Jews and Greeks dwelling in Ephesus; and fear fell on them all, and the name of the Lord Jesus was magnified. And many who had believed came confessing and telling their deeds.

SIGNS AND WONDERS IN NAME OF JESUS

As we listen to God and obey His voice, we must boldly step out and by faith use the awesome authority of the name of Jesus. When we do, we will experience signs and wonders in our daily life and ministry.

> Acts 4:29-31 Now, Lord, look on their threats, and grant to Your servants that with all boldness they may speak Your word, by stretching out Your hand to heal, and that signs and wonders may be done through the name of Your holy Servant Jesus.

And when they had prayed, the place where they were assembled together was shaken; and they were all filled with the Holy Spirit, and they spoke the word of God with boldness.

As we continue to use the authority and power of the name of Jesus, we too will shake our world with the presence and power of an awesome God.

The key for a victorious Christian life is found in the mighty name of Jesus.

We can walk with the same power as described in the book of Acts, when we join the early believers in using the authority of the name of Jesus.

QUESTIONS FOR REVIEW

1. Give two examples from the book of Acts, where the Apostles used the name of Jesus.

2. What is meant when we say the name of Jesus is like having a Power of Attorney?

3. In what challenges that you are facing right now, do you plan to experience victory by using the name of Jesus?

Lesson Twelve

Victorious Spiritual Warfare

EQUIPPED FOR BATTLE!

Divine Power

Now that we understand the eternal conflict and know our authority and our powerful weapons, we are equipped for powerful, victorious, overcoming warfare.

Paul wrote,

2 Corinthians 10:4 For the weapons of our warfare are not carnal but mighty in God for pulling down strongholds ...

Many have tried to enter warfare without this revelation. They have not understood the authority they have because of who they are in Jesus.

To them, spiritual warfare has become an intense, constant struggle with a powerful enemy. They have become occupied with the devil and his demons. The more their attention is centered on the devil and demons, the bigger, meaner, and more powerful they seem.

Defeated Enemy

The prophet Isaiah wrote of the future of Satan. He gave us a clear picture of his fate.

Isaiah 14:15-17 Yet you shall be brought down to Sheol, to the lowest depths of the Pit. Those who see you will gaze at you, and consider you, saying: 'Is this the man who made the earth tremble, who shook kingdoms, who made the world as a wilderness and destroyed its cities, who did not open the house of his prisoners?'

The people will stare at this one called Satan who is hopelessly defeated and humiliated. They will look in surprise at this one they thought was so big and powerful. They will see him cowering in disgrace. They will ask, "Is this the man ...?" "Is this the man who everyone has made such a big deal over?"

They will stare at this one who has been brought to nothing. They will look at him with scorn. They will see him in total defeat.

When we have a revelation of who we are in Jesus, we are no longer preoccupied with the devil. We are continually occupied with Jesus!

The devil is a defeated foe. His power has been destroyed. Jesus made a "zero" out of him. He has been disarmed, disabled and put to an open shame.

Brought to Nought

Hebrews 2:14b (Amplified Version) He [Himself] in a similar manner partook of the same [nature], that by [going through] death He might bring to nought and make of no effect him who had the power of death, that is, the devil.

We are at no disadvantage in dealing with the devil and his demons. We have been given power over all of the power of the enemy.

As we enter into warfare, it is to be from the position of confident assurance and faith that we are going to win. We are to enter into warfare from the position of knowledge of who we are in Jesus. We are not to plan on an intense struggle with a powerful enemy. We are, instead, to look forward to joyful victory as we demonstrate the fact that the devil is already defeated.

➢ The devil is not a "big deal."
➢ Jesus is the "**Big Deal!**"
➢ We can do all things through Him!

Philippians 4:13 I can do all things through Christ who strengthens me.

STEPS TO VICTORY

The power and authority of the believer is not a "toy" to accomplish our own selfish desires. We must be in complete harmony with the will of God.

Confession of Sin

If we are to be victorious in our spiritual warfare, we must first repent and confess our sins to God and receive His forgiveness. The apostle John told us how to do this.

1 John 1:9 If we confess our sins, He is faithful and just to forgive us our sins and to cleanse us from all unrighteousness.

Commitment

We must commit our lives, one-hundred percent, to Jesus as Lord of our lives.

Romans 12:1,2 I beseech you therefore, brethren, by the mercies of God, that you present your bodies a living sacrifice, holy, acceptable to God, which is your reasonable service. And do not be conformed to this world, but be transformed by the renewing of your mind, that you may prove what is that good and acceptable and perfect will of God.

Separation from World

We must separate ourselves from involvement with the affairs of the world.

2 Timothy 2:4 No one engaged in warfare entangles himself with the affairs of this life, that he may please him who enlisted him as a soldier.

Laying Aside our Desires

We must lay aside our own desires and be led by the Spirit of God. We, like Jesus, must say, "I only do what I see my Father doing."

John 5:19 Then Jesus answered and said to them, "Most assuredly, I say to you, the Son can do nothing of Himself, but what He sees the Father do; for whatever He does, the Son also does in like manner."

God has given every believer certain realms of authority over:

➢ Their marriages, children and families

➢ Where they live – neighborhoods, cities, nations

➢ Where they are sent by God to minister

Often we will not be released in our spirits to go into warfare over a stronghold of the devil in an area outside our God-given realm of authority. God wants the believers in that area to learn their authority and to pull down strongholds.

Have Attitude of Love

As soldiers, men and women of faith in God's army, we must not become arrogant and harsh in our attitude toward others.

Philemon 1:4,5 I thank my God, making mention of you always in my prayers, hearing of your love and faith which you have toward the Lord Jesus and toward all the saints.

We must be hard on the devil and demons, but we must continue to walk in love toward other people. We hate the devil, but we love people.

We must always remember that our authority as believers is not to take dominion over other people, but to take dominion over the devil and his demons.

As we walk in love toward God and other people, we are not to be continually thinking about warfare with the devil.

No Compromise

As we walk in a close relationship with God – without the mixture of compromise, sin or worldliness in our lives – God will warn us of Satan's strategies for our defeat by the operations of the spiritual gift of the discerning of spirits.

The closer we are to God, the more aware we will be of the presence of evil, deception, compromise or mixture when it comes.

We must keep our eyes on Jesus. If Satan or his demons get in the way – deal with them, resist them, cast them out – cast down thoughts and imaginations that are not of God. We are then to put our eyes back on Jesus as we praise Him for the victory.

2 Corinthians 2:14 Now thanks be to God who always leads us in triumph in Christ, and through us diffuses the fragrance of His knowledge in every place.

No Spiritual Specialist

In God's kingdom, it is not His plan that spiritual warfare and deliverance be accomplished by calling in, or going to, a specialist or a "high-powered demon chaser." Instead, as the apostle James wrote, every believer is to resist the devil.

James 4:7 Therefore submit to God. Resist the devil and he will flee from you.

THE ARMOR OF GOD

God has provided us with armor for the battle we are in. The apostle Paul did not write that we were to put on our armor; he wrote that we are to put on God's armor.

When the knights of medieval times put on their armor, and their helmets and dropped the visors over their faces, they all looked like powerful, muscular, dangerous warriors to the enemy. Regardless of the shortcomings of the body on the inside of that armor, they looked like mighty warriors.

When we put on God's armor, we look just like God to the devil. Then all we must do to win the battle is talk like God, walk like God, and act like God!

Our Power

We are to operate in God's mighty power. We are not to go into battle in our own strength.

Ephesians 6:10,11 Finally, my brethren, be strong in the Lord and in the power of His might. Put on the whole armor of God, that you may be able to stand against the wiles of the devil.

Our Struggle

v.12 For we do not wrestle against flesh and blood, but against principalities, against powers, against the rulers of the darkness of this age, against spiritual hosts of wickedness in the heavenly places.

Paul reminds us that our struggle is not with flesh and blood, but with rulers, authorities, and spiritual forces of evil. Our struggle is not in the areas of the natural world, but in the spiritual realm.

Our Armor

➤ *Belt of Truth*
➤ *Breastplate of Righteousness*
➤ *Feet Shod with Gospel*

vs.13-15 Therefore take up the whole armor of God, that you may be able to withstand in the evil day, and having done all, to stand. Stand therefore, having girded your waist with truth, having put on the breastplate of righteousness, and having shod your feet with the preparation of the gospel of peace.

Paul repeated the word "stand" three times. First he said that when the day of evil comes, we will be able to stand our ground. Then he said, after we have done everything, we should stand. Finally, he said, stand firm then with the breastplate of righteousness in place, and our feet shod with the preparation of the gospel of peace.

The truth is the Word of God. For it to be a protection for us, we must know what it says.

Our breastplate of righteousness is the righteousness of God. We are not required to be perfect, but we are required not to have known-sin in our lives for this breastplate to be in place.

Our feet are to be shod with the preparation of the gospel of peace. The preparation is our part and that is done by studying the Word of God.

Paul wrote to Timothy,

2 Timothy 2:15 Be diligent to present yourself approved to God, a worker who does not need to be ashamed, rightly dividing the word of truth.

> *Shield of Faith*
> *Helmet of Salvation*
> *Sword of the Spirit*

Ephesians 6:16,17 ... above all, taking the shield of faith with which you will be able to quench all the fiery darts of the wicked one. And take the helmet of salvation, and the sword of the Spirit, which is the word of God.

We are to use the shield of faith to extinguish the flaming arrows of the devil. The flaming arrows are thoughts, temptations, sicknesses and other strategies Satan throws at us. We are to extinguish them through faith in God and faith in His Word.

The helmet of salvation is put on when we receive salvation. This is a salvation that not only settles our eternal destiny, but one that restores us to all that we were created to be when we were created in God's image. The helmet of salvation allows us to renew our minds to the full revelation of our salvation.

Romans 12:2a And do not be conformed to this world, but be transformed by the renewing of your mind.

This renewing of the mind comes through the washing of our minds by the living "water" of God's Word as we read, study and meditate on it.

Ephesians 5:26 ... that He might sanctify and cleanse it with the washing of water by the word ...

We are given one offensive weapon and that is the sword of the Spirit which is the Word of God. Paul tells us more about the sword of the Spirit in the book of Hebrews.

Hebrews 4:12 For the word of God is living and powerful, and sharper than any two-edged sword, piercing even to the division of soul and spirit, and of joints and marrow, and is a discerner of the thoughts and intents of the heart.

The Word of God is our belt of truth, the covering for our feet and our sword! Can there be any doubt of the importance of studying the Word?

Victorious Praying

Once we have by faith, put on the full armor of God, we are to pray in the Spirit on all occasions.

Ephesians 6:18 ... praying always with all prayer and supplication in the Spirit, being watchful to this end with all perseverance and supplication for all the saints.

As we keep on praying in faith for all the saints, using our restored authority, we will see the strongholds of Satan fall. We will become valiant in battle and will rout the forces of Satan.

Hebrews 11:33,34 ...who through faith subdued kingdoms, worked righteousness, obtained promises, stopped the mouths of lions, quenched the violence of fire, escaped the edge of the sword, out of weakness were made strong, became valiant in battle, turned to flight the armies of the aliens.

EQUIPPED FOR WORK OF MINISTRY

Jesus said we were to go into all the world and preach the good news.

Mark 16:15 And He said to them, "Go into all the world and preach the gospel to every creature."

Isaiah talked about those who brought good news.

Isaiah 52:7 How beautiful upon the mountains are the feet of him who brings good news, who proclaims peace, who brings glad tidings of good things, who proclaims salvation, who says to Zion, "Your God reigns!"

Paul tells us that we are more than conquerors, that nothing can separate us from the love of God.

Romans 8:37-39 Yet in all these things we are more than conquerors through Him who loved us. For I am persuaded that neither death nor life, nor angels nor principalities nor powers, nor things present nor things to come, nor height nor depth, nor any other created thing, shall be able to separate us from the love of God which is in Christ Jesus our Lord.

Jesus tells us that from the time of John the Baptist until now, the kingdom of God is advanced by force.

Matthew 11:12 And from the days of John the Baptist until now the kingdom of heaven suffers violence, and the violent take it by force.

Paul tells us that the force is faith!

Hebrews 11:33 ... who through faith subdued kingdoms, worked righteousness, obtained promises, stopped the mouths of lions.

In Conclusion

*The work of Jesus is complete!
He has defeated Satan
and taken back everything
Satan took from Adam and Eve.*

*He has restored authority on this earth
to redeemed mankind,
those who are
His church — His mighty army!*

*Now it is up to us!
We are the ones to take the message
of this great salvation to all the world.*

*We are to forcefully advance
the kingdom of God.*

*We are to make the enemies
of Jesus His footstool.*

*We are to walk in authority
on this earth,
today!*

Verses To Memorize

Ephesians 6:12

For we do not wrestle against flesh and blood, but against principalities, against powers, against the rulers of the darkness of this age, against spiritual hosts of wickedness in the heavenly places.

1 Peter 5:8,9

Be sober, be vigilant; because your adversary the devil walks about like a roaring lion, seeking whom he may devour. Resist him, steadfast in the faith, knowing that the same sufferings are experienced by your brotherhood in the world.

John 10:10

The thief does not come except to steal, and to kill, and to destroy. I have come that they may have life, and that they may have it more abundantly.

Genesis 1:26

Then God said, "Let Us make man in Our image, according to Our likeness; let them have dominion over the fish of the sea, over the birds of the air, and over the cattle, over all the earth and over every creeping thing that creeps on the earth."

Genesis 3:15

And I will put enmity between you and the woman, and between your seed and her Seed; He shall bruise your head, and you shall bruise His heel.

Hebrews 2:14

Inasmuch then as the children have partaken of flesh and blood, He Himself likewise shared in the same, that through death He might destroy him who had the power of death, that is, the devil.

1 John 3:8

He who sins is of the devil, for the devil has sinned from the beginning. For this purpose the Son of God was manifested, that He might destroy the works of the devil.

Colossians 2:15

Having disarmed principalities and powers, He made a public spectacle of them, triumphing over them in it.

Revelation 1:18

I am He who lives, and was dead, and behold, I am alive forevermore. Amen. And I have the keys of Hades and of Death.

Ephesians 1:22,23

And He put all things under His feet, and gave Him to be head over all things to the church, which is His body, the fullness of Him who fills all in all.

Colossians 1:13

He has delivered us from the power of darkness and translated us into the kingdom of the Son of His love.

Romans 16:20

And the God of peace will crush Satan under your feet shortly. The grace of our Lord Jesus Christ be with you. Amen.

Luke 10:19

Behold, I give you the authority to trample on serpents and scorpions, and over all the power of the enemy, and nothing shall by any means hurt you.

Matthew 16:18,19

And I also say to you that you are Peter, and on this rock I will build My church, and the gates of Hades shall not prevail against it. And I will give you the keys of the kingdom of heaven, and whatever you bind on earth will be bound in heaven, and whatever you loose on earth will be loosed in heaven.

Revelation 12:11

And they overcame him by the blood of the Lamb and by the word of their testimony, and they did not love their lives to the death.

1 John 2:13,14

I write to you, fathers, because you have known Him who is from the beginning. I write to you, young men, because you have overcome the wicked one. I write to you, little children, because you have known the Father.

I have written to you, fathers, because you have known Him who is from the beginning. I have written to you, young men, because you are strong, and the word of God abides in you, and you have overcome the wicked one.

Philippians 2:9,10

Therefore God also has highly exalted Him and given Him the name which is above every name, that at the name of Jesus every knee should bow, of those in heaven, and of those on earth, and of those under the earth.

Books and Tapes
on the
Authority of the Believer
By A.L. and Joyce Gill

Destined for Dominion (Book)

From eternity past to eternity future, God has a plan for mankind. ***Destined for Dominion*** is an exciting, powerful book about the authority of the believer over the forces of evil. It explains the eternal conflict we are in and shows us how we can win!

Dr. Gary Greenwald wrote: This incredible book explodes with scriptural teaching and first-hand, true accounts of everyday spiritual warfare. Whereas Frank Peretti, in ***This Present Darkness***, peaked our interest in our spiritual battles and Satan's dark forces, A.L. Gill takes us on into real life training and victorious encounters with the enemy. I highly recommend this book.

Frances Hunter said: Once I started reading ***Destined for Dominion***, I didn't put it down until I completed it! It will bring a new spirit of boldness to the body of Christ!

Out! In the Name of Jesus (Book)

Out! In the Name of Jesus is a powerful self-guide to deliverance for those who are bothered by demon spirits. An important tool for Christian workers in its effective step-by-step approach to ministering deliverance.

People will be set free from demonic bondage! They will stay free because this book is based solidly on the Word of God.

Authority of the Believer Tape Album – *10 Hours of Audio or Video Teaching*

The life-changing revelation in these audio and video tapes reveals God's provision for mankind's victory and dominion over Satan. Beginning with the fall of Lucifer in eternity past, we see God's eternal purpose for mankind. When God created Adam and Eve, He said, "Let them have dominion!"

These exciting and powerful studies reveal to believers who they are in Jesus Christ, and how they can stop losing and start winning in the everyday battles of life.

This is a complete Bible study based on the manual, ***The Authority of the Believer***. It is excellent for personal study, home groups, or for use in Bible schools and churches.

Victory over Deception (Book)

Victory over Deception is a practical, compelling revelation of how to operate in the spiritual gift of discerning of spirits. You will learn how to distinguish the spirits of deception, witchcraft, false doctrines, control, and confidence games.

The truths in this book can help save your life as they have the lives of the author and her family.

Courses in This Series
By A.L. and Joyce Gill

The Authority of the Believer — *How to Quit Losing and Start Winning*

This life-changing study reveals God's provision for mankind's victory and dominion over Satan in the world today. God's eternal purpose for every believer was revealed at creation when God said, "Let them have dominion!" You will be released into a powerful new spirit of boldness as you discover how you can start winning in every struggle of life.

God's Provision for Healing — *Receiving and Ministering God's Healing Power*

This powerful teaching lays a solid Word foundation which releases the faith of the students to receive their own healing, walk in perfect health, and boldly minister healing to others. Many are healed as this revelation comes alive in their spirits.

Supernatural Living — *Through the Gifts of the Holy Spirit*

Every believer can be released into operating in all nine gifts of the Holy Spirit in their daily lives. From an intimate relationship with the Holy Spirit, each person will discover the joy of walking in the supernatural as the vocal, revelation, and power gifts are released.

Patterns for Living — *From the Old Testament*

God never changes! The way He deals with His people has been revealed throughout the Bible. What He did for His people in the Old Testament, He will do for His people today! You can learn the Old Testament truths to help you understand the New Testament.

Praise and Worship — *Becoming Worshipers of God*

Discover the joy of moving into God's presence and releasing your spirit in all of the powerful, fresh, biblical expressions of high praise and intimate worship to God. As you study God's plan for praise and worship, you will become a daily worshiper of God.

The Church Triumphant — *Through the Book of Acts*

Jesus announced, "I will build my Church and the gates of hell will not prevail against it." This thrilling, topical study of the book of Acts reveals that church in action as a pattern for our lives and ministries today. It will inspire us into a new and greater dimension of supernatural living as signs, wonders, and miracles are released in our daily lives.

The Ministry Gifts — *Apostles, Prophets, Evangelists, Pastors, Teachers*

Jesus gave gifts to men! These precious and important gifts are men and women God has called as His apostles, prophets, evangelists, pastors, and teachers. Discover how these gifts are being restored to His church, and how they function to equip the saints for the work of the ministry.

New Creation Image — *Knowing Who You Are in Christ*

This life-changing revelation will free believers from feelings of guilt, condemnation, unworthiness, inferiority and inadequacy, to be conformed to the image of Christ. It will release each believer to enjoy being, doing, and having all for which they were created in God's image.

Miracle Evangelism — *God's Plan to Reach the World — By John Ezekiel*

A powerful study which will release believers into becoming daily soul winners in the great end-time harvest through miracle evangelism. Like the believers in the book of Acts, we can experience the joy of reaching the lost as God confirms His Word through signs, wonders, and healing miracles.

Many of the manuals are available in other languages.
French, Korean, Russian, and Spanish.
There are also teaching tapes and videos that go with most of the courses.
Call Powerhouse Publishing for more information.
1-800-366-3119